By David Masters

Wonders of Salvage
When Ships Go Down
Divers in the Deep Seas
Crimes of the High Seas
S.O.S.
Tales of the Submarine War
Up Periscope
So Few
With Pennants Flying
On the Wing
Perilous Days
Glory of Britain
Conquest of Disease
Miracle Drug
Epics of Salvage

EPICS OF SALVAGE

Contents

First American Edition Published June, 1954

Reprinted December 1954

F
COP 1
9.3.58
350

EPICS OF SALVAGE

*Wartime Feats of the
Marine Salvage Men in World War II*

BY DAVID MASTERS

Boston
LITTLE, BROWN AND COMPANY

Foreword

AFTER the First World War, *Wonders of Salvage* revealed to many people a field of human endeavor that provoked profound interest because it was largely unknown. It is my privilege to describe in the present book some of the outstanding cases of marine salvage that occurred in the Second World War. This time the field widens from the seas around the coasts of Great Britain to those of the United States, the Middle East, and New Zealand. In these world-wide operations hundreds of ships were saved from destruction; and this book describes a variety of cases which show the remarkable ingenuity of salvage officers and crews and their unfailing courage when difficulties were rife and weather foul. For every case described in the following pages there are dozens of others equally interesting, and the officers and men mentioned are but a few of those who served the Allied cause in the same way with equal devotion. If readers come to realize how much we owe to these men, I shall count my task well done.

I am happy to record my thanks for the generous cooperation of the Admiralty Chief of Naval Information; the Port of London Authority; Mr. G. R. Critchley, C.B.E., of the Liverpool and Glasgow Salvage Association; the Bureau of Ships, Navy Department, Washington; the Merritt-Chapman and Scott Corporation, New York; the New Zealand Shipping Company; the Italian Naval Authorities; the United Salvage Proprietary, Melbourne; J. P. Williams and Associates, Melbourne; Mr. F. W. Sully, MM.I.C.E.; Commander G. J. Wheeler; Commander G. C. Evans; and others, without whose help this book could not have been written.

EPICS OF SALVAGE

CHAPTER I

The World's Greatest Salvage Feat

A WORKMAN with a burning torch that suddenly spurted flame among some kapok life-preservers led to the sinking of the largest liner in the world and the greatest feat of marine salvage ever performed. The French liner *Normandie* cost £8,000,000 to build. She exceeded by eleven feet the *Queen Mary's* length of 1018 feet, and when the United States requisitioned her on December 12, 1941 — a few days after the Japanese struck their treacherous blow at Pearl Harbor — for conversion into a troopship, her importance to the Allied cause could not be overemphasized. She was big enough and fast enough to move an army of men across the world at a speed running up to thirty knots. Though France had capitulated, this great liner conjured up by her genius might still fight for her under the new name of U.S.S. *Lafayette* and the guidance of American hands.

Workmen poured into her where she lay at Pier 88 in New York harbor and stripped her day by day of all her luxurious furniture and any unnecessary fittings. Her interior was transformed. Canvas bunks were fitted up for over 10,000 men. Blankets were provided for warmth and comfort. The galleys were packed with plates and cutlery and drinking vessels. Food of all sorts flowed into the big refrigerated compartments until they were stuffed with victuals.

In the grand lounge where the elite were wont to sit and chat in the spacious prewar days, some eleven hundred bales of kapok life preservers were stacked ready to be stenciled before being distributed throughout the ship, and it was here at two-thirty in the afternoon of February 9, 1942, that a workman with a torch touched a pile of these inflammable life preservers. In minutes the flames roared through the lounge, eating up everything in their way. Unhappily a strong wind created a forced draft which within sixty minutes turned the promenade deck into a blazing inferno, and in a short while the flames were shooting from the bridge and dense clouds of smoke were billowing from the boat deck and sun deck.

The New York Fire Department, whose fire fighters were soon on the spot, fought hard to prevent the flames from reaching the lower decks and attacking the pier. They poured cataracts of water into the burning decks. Several cargo doors happened to be open in the liner's side, and as the weight of water collected in the upper decks she became unstable and began to heel. Slowly, inexorably, as she canted, the open doors were brought nearer to the water until they slid under. The water gushed into her and twelve hours after the fire started she turned over on her port side and sank with her decks standing almost upright in the water and her keel submerged from end to end.

The American people, shocked by the losses inflicted by the German submarines along the Atlantic seaboard, were shaken by this latest disaster. Some criticism was heard, but it was overwhelmed by a strong desire to help. The letters which began to dribble into the Navy Department soon grew to a torrent. They came in by the sackful. Each letter was from some patriotic citizen who had ideas for refloating the *Lafayette*, and each was carefully read. Some contained good points, but among the crank ones was a suggestion for filling the ship with ping-pong balls, another thought the liner could be raised by stacking her tight with empty cans, while one writer, impressed by the buoyancy of ice, was of the opinion that ice blocks would bring the *Lafayette* to the surface.

None of these well-meaning people had the faintest idea of

the intricate problems involved. The great liner lay on her side in the harbor between Piers 88 and 90 while the tide lapped about her three enormous streamlined funnels that were each big enough to serve as tunnels for a couple of subway trains. People came along West Street and stared at the phenomenal sight, wondering what would be done. The experts did the same. From the biggest liner in the world the *Lafayette* had suddenly changed into the biggest problem in the world.

On February 24, a fortnight after she rolled over and sank, the Chief of the Bureau of Ships in the Navy Department in Washington called in Captain W. A. Sullivan, Supervisor of Salvage of the United States Navy and put him in charge of the overturned liner. Captain Sullivan promptly consulted the experts of the Ships Salvage Division of the Merritt-Chapman and Scott Corporation, who, since Merritt and Chapman had righted and raised the American liner *St. Paul* in New York harbor in the First World War, had grown into the largest marine salvage concern in existence. They were then dealing with many wrecks for the Navy Department. After his consultations Captain Sullivan decided to go ahead with the cutting away of the funnels and the whole of the superstructure to clear the decks in readiness for salvaging the ship.

At that time the Navy Department was undecided what to do with the wreck. A committee of experts was therefore appointed to consider the matter on the following terms:

(a) Should this vessel be raised or should it be disposed of as scrap in her present condition, and, if the latter, what method is considered the most practical?

(b) If it is determined to raise the vessel, when she is afloat should she be scrapped or should the consideration of her disposition after raising be left for study until she is afloat?

The experts began to consider the removal of the wreck from all angles. Should she be cut up for scrap and carted away piecemeal? The sheer weight of the hulk might make her dig down into the harbor bed, so they pondered the problem of cutting away as much as they could and letting the rest of the wreck bury itself. Directly they came to dwell on the future developments of the harbor, however, they realized that such a vast mass of metal buried in the mud and clay would be an obstruction that might create insuperable difficulties at some future date. On this point the omens were not favorable. When they came to work out the probable cost of cutting up the wreck, the sum assumed such colossal proportions as to make them abandon the idea.

Cutting her up being out of the question, they wondered whether they could build a giant cofferdam round her and deal with her that way. The building of the cofferdam would demand a vast amount of material, it would cost an immense sum and take a long time. Assuming that it were built and pumped out, they were still confronted with the problem of refloating the ship. Could they do it? The question was unanswered. They did not know. The time and money that such a project demanded coupled with the uncertainty of refloating the wreck made them discard the idea.

They came to consider the possibility of uprighting her in the same way that the liner *St. Paul* had been uprighted in New York harbor so many years ago with shear legs all along her hull. But the *Lafayette* was the biggest liner in the world and the *St. Paul* was no more than a third of her size. After due consideration, the committee rejected the suggestion as unsuitable.

In the end the committee decided to put their faith in pumps alone. They planned to seal all the openings in the ship below the water level, and divide the whole length of the ship from stem to stern into numerous compartments with watertight bulkheads, and gradually bring her upright and refloat her by pumping. It was a most complex operation of a magnitude never before attempted.

The committee worked fast. All their profound technical

knowledge was devoted to the common task of dealing with the mammoth wreck. Within three weeks the committee made its report:

(a) The vessel should be raised.

(b) Considering the uncertain future needs of the war effort, the committee feels that a decision as to whether the ship should be reconditioned and for what purpose should not be made at this time. Such a decision should await the development of future war conditions and needs as the salvage of the ship draws nearer. Since there is a possibility that the war emergency may make the reconditioning of the ship desirable, every reasonable effort should be made to expedite the salvage.

It was hoped that the salvage of the *Lafayette* could be carried out in less than two years, and that it would not cost more than five million dollars. This was an appalling price to pay in human endeavor and treasure for the action of one man with a burning torch.

The wreck of the liner was not the only problem which the committee had to take into account. Important as it was, and eager as the American people were to see something done about it, there was the menace of the German submarine that was killing ships right and left on the Atlantic seaboard. The committee could not ignore this problem. It was vital to the nation. The *Lafayette* was a long-term prospect. The immediate need was to get as many of the wrecked merchant ships back into service as soon as possible.

The United States was confronted with the same difficulties that assailed Great Britain at the outbreak of war — too few trained salvage officers to cope with the ships the Germans were slaughtering. Every salvage expert, naval and civilian, was wanted to counter the German attack on ships. To deal with the *Lafayette* would take hundreds of men and dozens of divers. The United States Navy did what the British Admiralty did — they started teaching centers to train salvage officers and divers, and the *Lafayette* became what was virtually a training school in which divers and salvage officers could gain practical experience.

Meanwhile Captain Sullivan cut down his demands for skilled technical men to a minimum. Captain John I. Tooker of the Merritt-Chapman and Scott Corporation was appointed the salvage officer, while Mr. A. C. W. Siecke, a naval architect and consulting engineer of the same corporation, was given the task of working out the intricate details of the great plan, the strength of the bulkheads, the stability of the ship, and many other things. Another technical officer of the same firm, Mr. M. C. Gilbert, who had specialized in underwater cutting and welding, was also called in to help.

In sinking, the bow of the *Lafayette* had swung out about 160 feet toward the opposite Pier 90, while her stern was only five feet from Pier 88. Under some of the boiler rooms about a third of the way from her bow she rested on a rock ledge that shelved away deeply into the subsoil in the direction of the river and left much of her length cradled in the mud. The crest of this rocky ledge which ran from pier to pier had been dredged to a depth of forty-six feet. The question arose whether the bed of the harbor would support this tremendous weight or whether she would sink imperceptibly in the mud and underlying clay until she reached bed rock. Some specialists were quickly called in to take sample cores of the harbor bed at certain depths. These cores were sent to Harvard University where they were tested by a scientist whose report was reassuring. That she was bearing hard upon the rock was proved when her stern in three months sank three feet deeper in the mud and pushed up her bow a little higher. Very concerned at the damage the rock might do, the salvors took every precaution in their power to ease the strain. However, they were in no position to discover whether the rock had damaged her hull until the time came to refloat her some eighteen months later.

When the divers came to explore the submerged half of the ship they found absolute chaos. In turning over, everything moveable had shot to the sunken side and alleyways and passages were choked with debris. Before any real work could be done, all this stuff had to be cleared. Things were wedged so tightly that the divers could not clear them without a struggle.

The divers themselves were afflicted with the most annoying handicaps. In the first place, the water was so muddy that they could see nothing when they were submerged. Submersible lights were useless. They were compelled to work by touch. If they had been able to stand upright when they were clearing the debris from the passages they would have counted themselves lucky. But they could not stand upright. The passages had plenty of headroom when the ship was afloat, but now that she was lying on her side the floors and ceilings had changed into walls and the walls had become the floors and ceilings, with the consequence that, as the passages were little more than three feet wide, the divers were compelled to kneel or crouch in very cramped positions in order to work. Imagine them crouching there in the dark, hardly able to move, grappling with the rubbish to clear it out of the way.

They ran the gravest risks as they penetrated into the liner. There were jagged pieces of metal waiting to trap them or cut their air pipes, masses of broken glass on which to come to grief. They did in fact move tons of broken glass from the wreck. What was much worse than the broken glass, however, was the fine spun glass used as insulation in the liner. These fine glass fibers worked into the hands and nothing could be done about it until they worked out naturally.

There was so much combustible material in the half of the ship remaining above water that the salvage officers were afraid of another fire. To obviate a further outbreak they ran a water main down to the wreck and installed the piping the whole length of the liner with vents at intervals to couple up hoses that would enable them to reach any part of the ship.

An all-around-the-clock fire watch was instituted under an officer from the New York Fire Department, who was appointed for the specific purpose of guarding against fires. Every man using a hydrogen cutter was accompanied by another with a fire extinguisher, whose duty it was to see that a fire was not started.

On top of all the other drawbacks which hampered the salvors was the fact that two of the city sewers flowed out into the harbor near the wreck. There was some talk of deflecting them, but this was not practicable, so the risk of gas collecting in the wreck was a real danger. To safeguard the workers it was necessary to institute a system of gas tests. Rescue apparatus and gas masks were installed throughout the wreck and compartments and chambers were tested before workers were allowed to enter. Hydrogen sulphide gas arising from decaying matter was sometimes found in deadly quantities, but the tests revealed it and prevented a tragedy.

Seven hundred men swarmed about the stricken monster above the surface, doing the many jobs necessary to prepare for the refloating. They took down all the partition bulkheads and removed every bit of furniture that they could lay their hands on. All the three-ply wood and other wood in the vessel was ripped out along with every combustible thing that could be found. While those above the surface dealt with things above water, there were from seventy to seventy-five divers clearing the ship under water right down to her skin.

Everything was sheared off the promenade deck to leave it flat, except that part of the superstructure on the outer edge of the wreck which was buried so deeply in the mud that it was impossible to get at it. The salvors were obliged to leave this to be dealt with at a later date.

As soon as the submerged parts of the ship were cleared, the divers began to prepare the way for the bulkheads that were to divide the wreck into fourteen compartments. Anything that stood in the way of a bulkhead was cut away until there was a clear run from the surface to the skin of the ship. It meant, of course, that each of the compartments had to be watertight, which in its turn meant that every pipe and opening large and small leading from one compartment to another had to be found and stopped. It seemed a never-ending job.

There was one thing which gave the divers a little help in their arduous duties. By studying the portion of the ship above water, they were able to take their measurements for the work they wished to do under water. Even so, it was necessary to check the measurements on the submerged parts of the ship, for sometimes fittings were found below which did not exist on the upper portion and these had to be dealt with. It was nevertheless a big advantage to be able to study the upper part of the liner to gain an idea of what the submerged part was like, for it assisted the divers to find their way about and warned them what they had to look for.

Every precaution was taken to insure the safety of the divers. The wreck was so huge, the passages so many. With dozens of divers creeping in a doubled-up position along the passages and groping about the various compartments in the dark, the risk of fouling their lines was never absent. On a task of this magnitude it would have been a miracle had no mishaps occurred. Slips did occur. Divers were often fouled, but they were always freed, and one of the finest tributes to those who supervised the work was that although on an average seventy divers were employed under water and seven hundred men above water, not a single life was lost during the whole operation.

When the liner capsized there were hundreds of portholes open on the side now under water as well as several cargo doors. The mud was squeezed up through the openings like toothpaste from a tube. In some compartments around the open cargo doors it was twenty feet deep and divers had to work completely buried in mud. In other cases it came up to the armpits or well up the thighs. It was estimated that about

15,000 tons of mud had penetrated through these openings. All of it had to be removed by the divers with their suction pumps or air lifts before they could get to the skin of the ship. The air-lift pump was used when the mud had caked. Air under strong pressure was delivered at the lower end of a big upflow pipe. The air naturally gushed to the surface, carrying the water with it. This strong flow of water to the mouth of the pipe washed away the mud in the neighborhood and carried it to the surface.

The main source of trouble, of course, was that the portholes and doors remained open, and while they were open the mud continued to come in. Yet it was essential to the success of the salvage plan that the portholes should be patched and the doors closed from the outside of the ship before she could be pumped out. The divers were barred from burrowing underneath her, while the pressure of the mud at these openings prevented anything from being passed through to the outside of the ship. The mud problem was more than a nuisance. It began to look as though the divers would have to remove half the mud in the harbor thereabouts before they could fix their patches. Fortunately it did not turn out to be quite so bad as that. By exercising all their skill and patience, the divers eventually consolidated the mud outside the portholes to such a degree that it became firm enough to hold back the ooze behind it. An aperture shaped liked a pudding basin was thus formed in the mud under each porthole, and the diver was able to fit a bed of rubber round the outer edge of each porthole and insert through the opening a Tooker patch that was hinged to fold in halves, whereupon the patch was opened and pulled up to the rubber bed. It was then screwed to a strongback — a metal bar — inside the ship at the diver's feet and sealed off with concrete to insure that it was watertight and strong enough to withstand all strains. When the time came to pump out the ship, the immense pressure of water outside would tend to squeeze the patch tightly against its rubber bed and as the patch was bigger than the hole it sealed there was no possibility of its being pushed into the interior of the ship. In this way the divers sealed 356 portholes and they also succeeded in closing and sealing 16 cargo doors.

The holes, large and small, to be sealed in the promenade deck to make it watertight were legion. The hatch openings, being large like the ship herself, demanded large patches to cover them. The biggest patch was fifty-four feet long and twenty-two feet wide. It was built on a float alongside the upturned promenade deck. By the time the shipwrights had completed it, the vast patch was three feet deep and weighed fifty-two tons. To make sure that it would be strong enough to withstand the pressure of the sea when pumping started, the salvage experts strengthened it with steel girders, the outer face of the patch being built of planks twelve inches wide by four inches thick.

The decks posed another problem to exercise the minds of the experts. Decks, as everyone knows, are made to walk upon. The girders and beams on which they are carried also serve to tie the ship together and prevent the hull from being crushed inwards by the pressure of the sea. Decks are quite strong enough to carry the heaviest load they will be called upon to bear, but they are not designed to take the place of the hull. Yet, in this case, the starboard hull of the ship had changed places with the deck which for half its width along its whole length was taking the place of the hull. So long as the ship was flooded and the water remained on both sides of the seven decks there was nothing to fear. The pressures were balanced. But to pump out the ship without taking precautions would have been to court catastrophe, for the decks, lacking the pressure of the water inside them to balance the pressure outside, would assuredly have collapsed.

To avoid that disaster and withstand the enormous load the promenade deck would have to bear when pumping began and the ship started to turn, the divers had to strengthen the deck with shores composed of great balks of timber. These were fixed in place by hammering home double wedges which made them absolutely tight. One by one these shores, weighted with rails, were lowered to the divers, who maneuvered them into place and wedged them home until they had installed a veritable forest of timbers. It seemed incredible that such work could have been done so accurately in the dark under the water by touch alone.

In constructing the bulkheads to divide the wreck into the compartments for pumping, the salvors used a weighted cradle to lower the main timbers for the frame on which the bulkhead was based. When these timbers were fixed into position, the building of the bulkhead proper started from the top with timbers that were tongued and grooved similar to matchboards. Each timber was clamped and lowered in slings to the divers, who manipulated it until the tongue of the timber was in perfect alignment with the groove in the timber above it. On the order of the divers, the men above hauled on both ends of the timber simultaneously until the tongue was forced home in the groove, whereupon the divers bolted each end to the main supports. After this they embedded the ends of the bulkheads in concrete to prevent any leakage.

For month after month they toiled away. Commodore Sullivan, to give him his present rank, was called upon to serve in the Mediterranean where he did wonderful work in supervising the removal of the wrecks from Naples harbor and other ports. His technical skill was invaluable to the Allies. His successor as Supervisor of Salvage in charge of the salvage operations on the *Lafayette* was Captain B. E. Manseau, USN.

The operations were carried on without respite. As soon as one shift finished their spell of duty, another shift came on. It was a non-stop task, lit up at night in the later stages by a string of powerful arc lights mounted from end to end of the starboard edge of the deck which was some fifty or sixty feet above the water level. Removing the funnels and masts, cutting off the bridge, taking out derricks, and clearing every-thing down to the promenade deck lightened the wreck by about five thousand tons. It was only one of many big jobs.

The last grand task before the biggest operation of all was the installation of the motor pumps in the fourteen water-tight compartments. It became a major battle with unexpected difficulties. The salvors calculated that there was a hundred thousand tons of water in the wreck. To deal with this huge weight and adjust the water levels in the various compartments in order to balance the ship and gradually turn her into an upright position demanded vast pumping power. The tech-nicians estimated that with forty ten-inch pumps, twenty-eight six-inch pumps, and twenty-five three-inch pumps they could deal with 40,000 tons of water an hour and accomplish all that they desired. To prevent the suctions of the pumps from being choked, they were protected by big square cages of strong steel mesh. Fixing them exactly where they were wanted in the different compartments was arduous and risky, so the experts planned to leave them in their original positions as long as possible without disturbing them. They were not prepared to ask the riggers to handle a pump twice if once would do.

Salvage pumps, of course, are among the mechanical mar-vels of the age; but even so they cannot perform impossibili-ties. The makers construct them to deliver their maximum output in certain conditions and in certain well-defined posi-tions. These motor-pumping units functioned best when they were standing upright. But it must not be overlooked that as the pumping progressed, the wreck would start to turn and the pumping units would of necessity turn with the wreck. This meant that if they started in an upright position they would slowly tilt and if the tilt became too acute they would cease to work. These pumps, however, were designed to work efficiently even if the units were sloping at an angle of fifteen degrees. The salvors took full advantage of this by mounting the pumping units on hinged platforms, the outer edges of which were suspended from chains which could be adusted to keep the pumps in a horizontal position as long as possible. This saved any amount of time and trouble in the final stages of the work, for the riggers merely had to alter a few links of chain instead of struggling to move the whole pump weighing nearly a ton and a half, as they were forced to do later when the depth of water was lowered in the wreck.

It was anticipated that the mud in which she had been resting for so long would tend to hold the *Lafayette* down. Nor did they forget that mass of superstructure on the edge of the deck which the divers were unable to remove because it was buried in the mud. This might anchor the wreck in the mud and stop her from turning. They were anxious to release her very gently. To loosen the mud beneath her they had fitted in numerous porthole patches the necessary pipes through which water and compressed air could be jetted to disintegrate the mud. They were afraid that if she broke away suddenly from her bed she might get out of control and suffer serious consequences.

The plan for pumping was most carefully worked out so that the liner could be controlled by adusting the weight of water in the watertight compartments. Long before the final stage was reached, the pumps were set in motion to enable the divers to locate and stop all leaks. This was grueling work. Leaks were continually manifesting in all sorts of unexpected places and compelling the divers to go to endless trouble to stop them. The multitudes of pipes that served for washing and sanitary purposes in the ship were a particular source of leakage, yet one by one they had to be found and plugged. From the first to last the divers fixed nearly five thousand patches, wedges, and plugs to make the ship tight.

During the last fortnight in July, Captain Tooker made a pumping test in each of the watertight compartments. These

were designed to reveal the remaining leaks. They did —
and gave the divers the chance of putting the finishing touches
to their work. The tests did not disturb the wreck at all. She
remained quiescent. There was not a tremor. On August 2
it was decided to make a pumping test in all the compartments
together, and as the water gushed from the outflows on the
upper part of the promenade deck the water in the submerged compartments was lowered from one to two feet
below the level of the water outside the ship. This was actually the big dress rehearsal for the final pumping operations.
For forty-eight hours the levels of the water inside the ship
were maintained below the outside level. All the time the
divers were busy treating cracks and seams with sawdust to
seal them effectively.

Satisfied with the test, Captain Manseau and Captain Tooker
set the pumps in motion at one o'clock on August 4, 1943, to
begin the task of pumping out the wreck and turning her upright. In four and a half hours the water was reduced in some
compartments by nine feet, and in others by nine and a half
feet. In the meantime the tide had risen five feet, so the water
inside the ship was fourteen feet below the outside water
level and the patches were under severe strain. The cataracts
of water pouring from the wreck seemed to make little difference. Visually there seemed to be no alteration at all, but
the measuring instruments installed on the deck gave accurate
details of her slightest movement. The experts found at the
end of the day that the deck had moved little more than half
an inch. Trifling though it was, it was an earnest of things to
come.

Work continued throughout the next twenty-four hours.
Extra stays were added to strengthen the deck against the
strain, and renewed pumping lowered the water level in the
compartments another six inches. By eight o'clock on the
morning of August 6 the inside water level was fifteen feet
below that outside where the tide had another four feet to rise.

An hour and a half later, under the lift of the tide, the salvage officer felt the mammoth wreck begin a slight roll. It told him that all was well, that by working their pumps according to plan and filling the starboard tanks on the upper part of the liner with several thousand tons of water at the propitious moment they could roll the wreck back into an upright position and float her.

Their plan was sadly disrupted on August 9 when they struck bad trouble. It was in compartment 16, just where the wreck was sitting on the rocky ledge. Although the pumps in the compartment were run continuously all day they could not bring down the water level. The water poured in as fast as it was pumped out. Divers started an intensive search for the leaks. Next day they began searching outside the ship as well as inside, by which time the stern was definitely afloat. The search for the leaks went on, and the following afternoon the divers found two splits in the plates within eight feet of each other. They treated one with rags and sawdust in an attempt to seal it and rammed rolled sacks into the other, while pumping went on all the time.

On August 13 a diver found a hole a yard wide in one of the tanks in boiler room No. 2. The dimensions of the hole were given to the shipwrights who made a Tooker patch for it in a couple of hours, and fifteen minutes later the divers fixed it in place. Using oakum and sawdust, the divers strove methodically to stop the leaks inside the compartment. By nine o'clock that evening Captain Tooker had five ten-inch motor pumps working there in an effort to cope with the flood.

For the next five weeks the salvors waged a ceaseless battle to seal off the leaks and bring this compartment under control. Divers outside the wreck, using long poles, pushed bags of sawdust and rags down into the mud as close to the damage as they could get in the hope that some of these would be sucked into the fractures and help to stop the inflow. Divers inside the ship built a containing wall by piling up bags of cement and filling the gap between the wall and the hull with a hundred tons of concrete to seal the damaged plates. As soon as the concrete hardened, a pumping test indicated that these measures had been successful. Those who had striven so hard to overcome the trouble watched the level of the water fall foot by foot until it was ten feet lower. For a while it hung at this level, then all of a sudden it began to rise again. Swift investigation disclosed new fractures between the boilers and the tanks in a space so narrow that the divers could not get at them.

While the salvage experts were struggling to control this compartment, they set in train the part of their plan to bring the ship upright by pumping water into the starboard tanks so that the weight, pressing down, would tend to turn the ship the right way up. A hundred tons or so in this tank, over two hundred tons in that, two hundred tons in the next and so on, filling each according to its capacity, began to help the turning movement of the liner. There were many tanks, and as they were filled the water in them began to assume a massive weight. The air and water jets were set to work beneath the liner to loosen the mud, though she did not stick as they expected. At length, by pumping to adust the water in the various compartments and by filling the starboard tanks with 2800 tons of water, they brought her from her capsized position of 79.5 degrees to about 25 degrees. This was fine progress.

Before continuing this turning operation, Captain Tooker sent the divers down outside to investigate her position on the ledge of rock. It was well that he did so, for the divers found that if she were turned a little more her plates would make contact with some jagged edges of rock that would assuredly do a great deal more damage, so the turning movement was discarded for the time being and efforts were redoubled to gain control of the flooded compartment.

The salvors accordingly decided to fill the double bottom with eight hundred tons of concrete to stop up the fractures as much as possible. They did not expect the concrete to block all leaks, but they anticipated that it would serve as an effective barrier to objects of any size dumped into the sea in the vicinity. The divers then placed hundreds of sacks of rags and pushed dozens of mats and mattresses into the mud thereabouts. As soon as the pumps were started up in the compartment, the water rushing through the leaks carried into the holes some of the mattresses and bags of rags which checked the leakage to a considerable extent. It was by no means enough, for thirteen ten-inch pumps working at full pressure were still needed to pump out seven feet of water in the compartment and hold it at that level, and so thousands of tons of water were still pouring in every hour.

Eventually, by adding extra shores to strengthen the bulkheads, the compartments adjacent to the flooded one were pumped down farther to give the wreck more buoyancy that would help to lift her clear of the jagged rock. Then the salvors began to exert a big strain on her bow mooring and kept it up for two days. In that time it shifted her bow sixteen feet, eased her clear of the dangerous rock and brought her fractured plates over the cache of mattresses and bags of rags which checked the inflow still more. At long last, after the holes in the hull had swallowed three thousand bags of rags along with mats and mattresses, the pumps were able to gain control, and the battle was won.

On September 13, 1943, as the tide reached its peak, the *Lafayette* floated safely off the bottom. She had a big list of 25 degrees and looked very lopsided, but the salvage officers of the United States Navy and the Merritt-Chapman and Scott Corporation had accomplished the biggest marine salvage feat ever undertaken. In a few weeks all the material weighing down her port side was removed, all her machinery was cleaned and sprayed to protect it and she was brought to an even keel before being towed in triumph to dry dock, with aircraft dipping in salute and her decks thronged with cheering men who had helped to write a new page of salvage history.

CHAPTER II

Mysterious Wrecks

WHEN Hitler boasted in the early days of the war of a secret weapon against which there was no defense, no one knew what it portended. There was little reason to doubt that Hitler himself regarded it as a war-winning weapon, but what it was remained for a time unknown. There was nothing to be done in the face of these threats but to allow Hitler to reveal his hand.

There was not long to wait. On October 5, 1939, barely a month after the outbreak of war, the Brocklebank steamer *Marwarri*, carrying many antiaircraft guns that were earmarked for fighting off the pending German air raids, was steaming along the Bristol Channel when she was mined. There was tremendous damage to the deck; the engine room was flooded, as was No. 5 hold, while four other holds began to fill. This was actually the first war casualty with which the Liverpool and Glasgow Salvage Association had to deal after their appointment as Admiralty Agents. At once tugs were sent out from Swansea, the southern base of the west coast area, and they managed to get the ship in tow and put her on the shelving beach near Mumbles Head according to plan. At high water her stern was submerged about three or four feet while her bow was above the surface.

Mine damage usually follows a recognized pattern that is familiar to experts. In this case the salvage officers would have been fairly safe in assuming that the hull of the *Marwarri* was fractured and holed in the engine room and No. 5 hold; consequently it was just a question of finding out the size of the hole and deciding how to deal with it. The divers moved slowly about the sea bed examining the hull of the steamer, but the more they examined her the more puzzled they became. They expected to find a gaping hole in her, but to their surprise they could find no trace of one. The fractures normally responsible for the flooding of engine room and holds were not there. The shock of the explosion had loosened many rivets, but this could not account for the flooding of the ship. She must have suffered extensive damage to flood as quickly as she had done, yet the divers could find no indication of it. The flooding of the *Marwarri* was most mysterious.

The very next day the *Lochgoil*, of the Royal Mail Lines, pulled out of Newport in Monmouthshire and was steaming along the Bristol Channel when she also was mined. Again the tugs came out from Swansea, got their towing wires aboard, and hauled her to the beaching ground near the Mumbles. She must have been pretty badly hit, for she was about ten feet lower in the water fore and aft than when she drew away from the quay.

The salvage officer noted with astonishment the tremendous damage to the deck. It was far worse than in the case of the *Marwarri*. In both cases it was very unusual for a steamer striking a mine to suffer so much damage on deck. Generally the hull and holds took the impact of the explosion and showed most signs of damage. This second case within twenty-four hours deepened the mystery. It completely baffled the expert salvage men who were dealing with the ships.

As soon as possible the salvage squad maneuvered their pumps into the engine room and No. 5 hold of the *Marwarri*. They put in a battery of three mighty twelve-inch pumps which between them could suck out over 2500 tons of water an hour, and among the other holds they distributed three more pumps that could each deal with about 180 tons of water an hour, so the combined pumping capacity was over 3000 tons an hour. These pumps were not long in reducing the depth of water in the flooded ship.

As the depth decreased the divers were able to examine the interior to clear up the mystery of her flooding. Not a casting attached to the hull of the ship was unbroken, and through all these broken pipes the water had flooded the ship. It was a form of damage that had never been experienced before, and it provided a puzzle for the salvage officers as well as for the Admiralty.

After the divers had plugged all the holes they could find, the pumps were put to work and the steamer was refloated on the rising tide. The engine room was in a dreadful mess, but the queer thing was that the engines were not seriously damaged.

A careful examination of the *Lochgoil* disclosed the same peculiar and unusual damage as in the *Marwarri* — the fracturing of the castings by the shock of the explosion. Many mines had wrecked many ships before, but here was something quite new, a mine which seemed to have a specific effect upon the ship's castings. It was evidently a new type of mine, though how this effect was created, nobody knew.

While officers were puzzling over the problem at the Admiralty, the salvage men were grappling with the stranded vessel. She had considerable buoyancy at the bow and stern, but amidships she was sagging and burying herself in the beach. The result was that as the tide rose and lifted her bow and stern, the weight of water holding her down amidships threatened to break her in halves.

Above all things, that was what the salvors wished to avoid. The sea was washing in and out of the engine room and No. 3 hold, and the divers found her plates were badly fractured on both sides of the hull. There were well-marked indications that the ship would break in two if the ends continued to rise with the tide while the midships portion sank deeper into the shingle.

In marine salvage circles this action is known as "sagging," while if a ship is caught with her flooded bow and stern in deep water while her middle rests on a sandbank or rock, the action of tearing her apart from the top downwards is known as "hogging." Both hogging and sagging are anathema to the salvage men, and they tried all the tricks they knew to prevent the ship from breaking.

At the time the *Lochgoil* was run aground the tides were at the neap, rising no more than ten feet. The spring tides would rise and fall twenty-nine feet. If the bow and stern strained upward for twenty-nine feet while the midships portion of the ship sat on the bottom, she could not avoid being torn in two.

The salvage men worked quickly to escape disaster. While the divers patched the fractures in the hull as far down as they could reach, their colleagues got busy with their pumps and started to suck the water out of the flooded engine room to lighten her as much as possible amidships. Removing 4000 tons of water an hour is as good as removing 4000 tons of cargo or machinery, so owing to the buoyancy fore and aft they were able to haul her a little farther up the beach.

Unfortunately it was not enough. Had they been able to pump out more water to increase her buoyancy amidship, they might have been able to tow her still higher up the shelving beach to escape spoiling some of the cargo in order to save the ship.

They were salvage men with a long tradition to uphold. Their association had been created for the sole purpose of saving the underwriters, who spent their lives insuring ships and cargoes, as much as possible whenever a ship got into trouble. Now they brought their lighters alongside and started to transfer the cargo of the *Lochgoil* to mitigate the loss and lighten the vessel, entering with zest into their dual task of salving cargo and ship.

For the five days since they had arrived at the wreck they had toiled unceasingly. Each tide rose a little higher. They dared not allow the bow and stern to swing up on the spring tides to exert all their tremendous force on the weakened portion of the ship where she was fractured. It was imperative to keep the bow and stern on the bottom. The only method of doing that was to flood the holds with sufficient water to rob them of their buoyancy. Strange as it seems, the salvors decided to sink the ship in order to save her.

Working against time, the divers cut holes through the hull of the vessel to admit the sea into each of the holds. Over these holes they fitted valves that were actuated by rods from the deck, so they could admit just as much water as they wanted and then shut it off. Thus they let in the sea to keep the entire ship on the bottom to relieve the strain on the weakened keel. For the moment the ship was safe and all danger of her breaking in two was averted.

With that problem out of the way, they concentrated on many others that remained. The deck of the ship was severely damaged, but all salvage men need is sufficient power to work a derrick or winch and they can soon reduce chaos to order. In this case they were handicapped by the lack of winches. The bedplates of all the winches were broken. Not a single deck structure was intact. Normally the salvors were sure to find a winch or derrick and some source of power in the ship herself, but in this case everything was knocked out. It was no good installing a portable electric generator or bringing steam through a pipe from a vessel alongside. Not a winch would work.

At low tide the salvage ship was dwarfed as she floated beside the *Lochgoil* like a two-day-old cygnet beside a swan. The sides of the wreck towered so high above the salvage ship that it was impossible for her to use her derrick to lift wreckage and haul it out of the way except for a spell at high water. This meant that the salvage men were obliged to manhandle the wreckage. Then the fuel oil covered everything with filth and prevented the divers from locating many of the leaks.

Little by little they stopped the holes, plugging and patching the fractured valves leading through the hull of the ship. Several refrigerated holds and compartments gave them a lot of trouble before they were sealed.

As the moon waned, the seas receded until the day came when the tide was low enough to enable the divers to get at the bulkhead between the flooded engine room and No. 3 hold. They found several fractures which exercised all their skill and patience.

Operating their giant pumps to reduce the water in the engine room, they learned that pipe after pipe was smashed as though someone had been around hitting them with a hammer. Each broken pipe meant a leak to be stopped. At one point they located five pipes through which water was pouring into the engine room.

Plugging pipes in the bottom of the ship which were open to the sea was not enough. When the time came to refloat the *Lochgoil* those plugs would be subjected to enormous pressure as the whole weight of the ship floated on them. Her every movement would make the sea exert a great upthrust on the undersides of the plugs, thus tending to force them out. The salvage men countered this risk in the only possible way. Driving home their plugs, they rammed them securely in place by fitting balks of timber between the tops of the plugs and the underside of the engine-room platform, so the plugs could not move without shifting the steel platform.

During these operations, other members of the team were busy burning away split and twisted plates on the bridge and decks and replacing them with new plates which were welded and strengthened with bars of steel ten inches wide and four inches thick. To stiffen the ship and stop her from breaking in two, they welded three great bars of steel forty feet long on each side of her to give her rigidity, performing this feat as though they were working in an engineering shop ashore instead of in the open sea.

At length, with all pumps and air compressors working to capacity, they managed to gain sufficient buoyancy in No. 3 hold to refloat the *Lochgoil* on November 28 and tow her to dry dock.

The engine room was a maze of fractured castings, bedplates of engines and compressors, columns, cast-iron pipes and bends — it was an orgy of broken castings, a marine Humpty-Dumpty that one would have sworn all the king's horses and all the king's men could not put together again. Yet they put her to rights eventually and made her as good as new. But never again did the *Lochgoil* go to sea, for when the rejuvenated ship made her maiden voyage it was as the *Empire Rowan*.

By the time they brought the *Lochgoil* into dry dock the mystery of the fractured castings and the unusual deck damage were mysteries no longer. These effects were due to Hitler's secret weapon, the magnetic mine, against which he boasted that there was no defense. He may have believed it. Whether the German scientists really believed there was no answer to the magnetic mine remains uncertain, but if they did, it was fortunate for the inhabitants of Great Britain that they were mistaken.

While the salvage men were struggling in Mumbles Bay to salve the *Marwarri* and *Lochgoil*, one ship after another began to founder in the Thames estuary through being mined. The Lords of the Admiralty were worried, for in channels that were carefully swept free of mines a ship would meet disaster a few hours later. If the mines were laid by submarine, it meant that a German U-boat had managed to find a way through the British defenses to perform the task. Whether a German submarine had in fact managed to get through to the mouth of the Thames was a matter for conjecture. The mines were laid. The ships were sunk. But it was by no means certain that a submarine was involved.

In technical circles it was known that towards the end of

the First World War the British Navy was experimenting with a new type of mine that was actuated by a magnet. When a huge body of metal such as a ship came within range of this mine, it moved a delicately poised magnetic needle which detonated the mine. A good deal of work was done on this mine by those naval specialists who became known as back-room boys, because they kept out of the limelight.

At the same time that they were carrying out these experiments with magnetic mines, their scientific minds naturally began to consider possible ways of countering the menace. Therefore the magnetic mine and its problems were not exactly new to the British Admiralty. It possessed the reports of the experiments carried out a generation ago and was lucky enough to have on its staff scientists who had studied many of the problems involved. In the circumstances it was not surprising that a feeling began to grow in the Admiralty that the new peril which was sinking ships in the Bristol Channel, the Thames estuary and other places might be a magnetic mine. There was no certainty. It was just a theory, based on the past work of British naval experts.

The mounting toll of ships in the mouth of the Thames began to look sinister, as though the channels to the Port of London were in danger of being blocked by wrecks. Sir Winston Churchill, who was then First Lord of the Admiralty, was very concerned at the sinkings, for none knew better than he that England's existence depended upon the merchant ships which fetch and carry. One bleak November day the secret weapon of Hitler attained a success that shook Churchill — no fewer than six merchantmen were mined at the mouth of the Thames. The slaughter of ships on such a scale had never occurred since the war started, and the seriousness of the sinkings was increased because the Admiralty had no exact evidence of the cause.

The Germans did not confine their attacks to particular areas. They sowed their mines at places far apart to engender the feeling that no place was secure. Nor were their victims confined to merchant ships, for they dealt a harsh blow to the Royal Navy in November 1939 by sinking two destroyers, while two others just managed to limp into port. If this was bad, worse followed on November 21, 1939, when the cruiser *Belfast* which had not long been completed was severely damaged in the Firth of Forth. The bad news that the cruiser had been crippled was known in most British newspaper offices next day, but in the national interest a strict naval censorship forbade publication of it. By some secret method the news was conveyed to the United States where it was published and broadcast on Friday, November 24, causing considerable consternation at the Admiralty which rightly sought to conceal such losses from the enemy. Then, on December 4, the battleship *Nelson*, far away on the northeast coast of Scotland, set off a mine in her hiding place at Loch Ewe, a bitter blow that was most wonderfully covered up by the extreme reticence of all who knew of it. On this occasion tongues were stilled.

By that time, however, the technicians at the Admiralty were no longer groping in the dark about the cause of the trouble, for on the night of November 22, the day after the cruiser *Belfast* was mined, a keen man on the lookout for German aircraft at Shoeburyness, a few miles from Southend, heard an enemy plane approaching and saw dropping from it something from which a parachute opened as it floated gently down into the Thames. A report was at once telephoned to the Admiralty who promptly ordered Lieutenant Commander J. G. D. Ouvry and Lieutenant Commander R. C. Lewis to report to the Admiralty without delay. Both officers were experts on mines, and their knowledge of fuses and the way mines were detonated was probably as great as that of any living man. They rushed to the Admiralty where they were interviewed by Churchill and Admiral Sir Dudley Pound, who explained what had happened at Shoeburyness and mentioned the importance of recovering the mine to see how it worked.

All knew the danger, none better than the two naval officers. Quietly they explained what they proposed to do and how they proposed to do it, and by two o'clock in the morning they were speeding along the road to Shoeburyness. Long before dawn they were wading over the filthy mud flats with a small lamp to reach the mine. The tide runs out so far at the mouth of the Thames that it uncovers immense stretches of mud. The man who saw the mine fall, however, had already marked the position, and the mine was located lying in the ooze about a quarter of a mile from the shore.

By the light of the lamp they looked it over and discussed it while the waters lapped toward them and slowly covered their quarry. Buoying it, they set guard over it and withdrew. It was high water at London Bridge that morning at 11:18 Greenwich time, in the intervening hours they worked out in the most meticulous detail a plan for withdrawing the fuse of the mine to render it harmless. They knew they were risking death. They also knew how much this mine jeopardized the safety of the country. It was the unknown factor that had baffled the Admiralty, and the enemy had delivered it into their hands.

Lieutenant Commander Ouvry with Chief Petty Officer C. E. Baldwin and Lieutenant Commander Lewis with Able Seaman A. L. Vearncombe stood on the beach at Shoeburyness that afternoon watching the tide ebb until the mine was uncovered. Another mine was found some distance away. They had worked out and discussed each detail of their proposed operations. They had secured special tools that would not deflect a magnet, if it was indeed a magnetic mine, and they had arranged to explain every movement before it was made so that two of the party at a safe distance could note down the movements and record their mistake — if they happened to explode the mine and blow themselves to pieces.

Electing to make the first attempt, Ouvry and Baldwin waded through the mud to the mine. They listened carefully to assure themselves that there was no time fuse at work. All was silent. Then step by step they called out what they were going to do and did it. Lewis and Vearncombe repeated the operations as they made a note of them to insure their accuracy.

The mine was very heavy. It lay partly on the fuse, and before Ouvry and Baldwin could tackle their task they were obliged to move it round to allow them to get at the fuse. Carefully they worked away, not knowing from second to second whether they were about to be killed, describing each action before they took it, listening to the voices of their comrades repeating the words.

Having removed the fuse, they straightened up with relief and imagined that their dreadful ordeal was over. Their companions joined them to give a hand in removing and loading the mine. As they began to shift it, they were startled to see another fuse in the bottom of the mine. This was a contact fuse, designed to detonate the mine if it struck anything hard, thus destroying the evidence that it was a new-type magnetic mine if it happened to fall on land. Taking a breather, they did their best to remove it; but it was difficult to manage and eventually it took the combined efforts of all four men to make the mine safe.

The story of their sublime courage has been told in greater detail before, and it will be told many times again so long as men recognize a supreme heroism that springs not from the heat of battle, but from a calm acceptance of fearful risks most carefully weighed.

Winston Churchill in the first volume * of "The Second World War," wrote of their feat:

That evening Ouvry and his party came to the Admiralty to report that the mine had been recovered intact and was on its way to Portsmouth for detailed

* *The Gathering Storm.*

examination. I received them with enthusiasm. I gathered together eighty or a hundred officers and officials in our largest room, and made Ouvry tell his tale to a thrilled audience, deeply conscious of all that was at stake. From this moment the whole position was transformed. Immediately the knowledge derived from past research could be applied for devising practical measures for combating the particular characteristics of the mine.

Before long, ships were protected from this menace by degaussing, which consisted of fitting an electric cable round the hull of a ship and passing through it an electric current. Lacking enough cable in the country for their purpose, those who fitted the ships started by using five hundred miles of cable a week while urging the manufacturers to give them three times as much. How the cable-makers turned out thousands of miles of cable and how thousands of ships were thus protected from magnetic mines was one of the outstanding feats of the war.

Experiments proved that the best way of sweeping magnetic mines was for a minesweeper to tow behind it long lengths of electric cable, known to the crews as tails, through which a current could be passed to blow up the mine. Unfortunately the cable suitable for this purpose would not float and the problem of making the cable buoyant seemed to be insuperable. It happened that Henly's Tire and Rubber Company made not only this type of cable, but also tennis balls. "Why not combine the two and make the tennis balls support the cable?" thought their research manager.

They did. They compressed tennis balls round the cable to make it float. Tennis players who found difficulty in obtaining tennis balls during the war will understand the reason when they know that twenty-three million tennis balls were used to make a million yards of floating cable for detonating magnetic mines.

That was no love game.

CHAPTER III

The Secret Naval Disaster

INSTEAD of a gentle tap on the door to herald a morning cup of tea, the sleeping people on the harbor front at Gibraltar were wakened at six o'clock in the morning by the sound of a big explosion, followed by another and another. The sentries on the Rock and the sailors on watch saw the tanker *Denbydale* sink with a broken back while the merchantman *Durham*, a fine cargo ship of 10,000 tons, and the *Fiona Shell*, a storage tanker, slowly foundered. That morning of September 19, 1941, the Italian Navy proved that it could still strike hard in spite of its losses at Taranto and Matapan. It was Prince Giulio Valerio Borghese, a descendant of an ancient Sienese family which has played a large part in Italian history, who carried the three human torpedoes, each ridden by two men, that were launched from the deck of the submarine *Scire* to run the gantlet of the Gibraltar defenses and make that daring attack.

A month earlier the enemy had made their first attempt on the shipping in Gibraltar Harbor with two other human torpedoes, but the electric batteries on which they ran had flickered out and frustrated the attempt. The second time they succeeded. Escaping ashore, the six Italians induced the Spanish authorities to turn a blind eye and allow them to return to Italy.

Men with long memories recalled that an earlier generation of Italian seamen had ridden astride torpedoes to attack the Austrian fleet off the coast of Dalmatia during the 1914–1918 war. Now a second generation was showing the same spirit.

The repercussions of the explosions in Gibraltar Bay penetrated to the other end of the Mediterranean where the famous battleship *Queen Elizabeth* and her consort *Valiant* were moored in Alexandria Harbor. The fleet air arm's attack on the Italian fleet in Taranto Harbor on November 11, 1940, with the torpedoing of three battleships as well as other damage, and Admiral Cunningham's victory at Matapan on March 24, 1941, which led to the destruction of three Italian cruisers and the immobilization of the rest of the Italian Navy, gave the Royal Navy the surface supremacy of the Mediterranean. But Admiral Cunningham was too wise to underrate the enemy. This attack on Gibraltar made it plain that though the Italian naval authorities were chary of risking their remaining ships, Italian seamen were still glad to risk their lives for their country.

More than willing to take chances that promised decisive results, as in the Battle of Matapan, Admiral Cunningham was taking no risks with the *Queen Elizabeth* and the *Valiant* while they were in harbor. To make doubly sure that the anchorage was safe, a special check was made on the defenses of Alexandria Harbor.

While the Italians were concentrating their attacks on Gibraltar, using the *Olterra* interned in Spanish waters as a base for their two-man torpedoes, they planned to strike at the British warships in Alexandria Harbor. Their first ship was wiped out in an air attack. Their second effort ended in the capture of all on board, among them one of the inventors of the new weapon — the other inventor was captured during a vain attack on Malta, but neither talked. The third attempt was launched on December 14, 1941, when Prince Borghese took his submarine *Scire* out of Leros in the Dodecanese with three two-man torpedoes housed in big cylinders on her deck and ten men to operate them, four being reserves. These specialists were clever swimmers whose training had been long and arduous.

They had worked as teams to find out the idiosyncrasies of their craft, practicing their code of underwater signals by touch until their reactions were automatic. They were well-drilled in taking their craft up and down or ahead and astern, stopping her as desired to detach her 600-pound nose of high explosive and attach it to the bottom of a ship.

The specialists in this branch of the Italian Navy nicknamed their torpedoes "pigs," while in the Royal Navy they were known as "chariots," and as chariots we shall refer to them hereafter. The Italian chariot was shaped like a torpedo which was twenty-one feet long and three feet in diameter. It had a propeller astern and two bucket seats let into the hull on which the men sat astride wearing light watertight suits and breathing masks, with an oxygen container on their backs which enabled them to breathe under water for considerable periods. The torpedo was packed with intricate machinery and propelled by batteries which gave it a range of twelve miles, while it was equipped with tanks that could be flooded or blown for diving or surfacing. Its maximum diving depth was one hundred feet, and in making an attack it was stopped on the bottom as near as possible to the ship to allow the mechanic to dismount and help his companion to detach the warhead and sling it under the bottom of the ship by attaching clips to the bilge keel.

Leros was some 430 miles from Alexandria in a straight line. But it was by no means a straight course that the *Scire* was able to follow, for there were British minefields specially laid to trap marauding enemy submarines and Prince Borghese had to navigate the *Scire* with circumspection to avoid them. Submerging by day to keep out of sight, he made what progress he could on the surface at night. He was determined not to be caught and destroyed like the others.

The attacking teams were well briefed. Italian reconnaissance aircraft had reported that two battleships of the *Queen*

Elizabeth class and an aircraft carrier as well as cruisers and other ships were lying snugly at anchor in Alexandria Harbor. The attackers had studied the silhouettes of the British battleships until they could recognize them in the dark, which was exactly what they would have to do. If the tragic end of the previous men obtruded occasionally into their thoughts, they probably found some solace in the fact that many of the Gibraltar attackers had managed to escape through Spain, and their own chances of getting away were at least as good. Their plan of escape was to swim ashore after carrying out their mission and make their way in the guise of French seamen to Rosetta where another submarine would wait on the nights of December 24 and 26 to pick them up at a fixed rendezvous. Lieutenant de la Penne was detailed to attack one battleship, the *Valiant*, Captain Marceglia was to attack the other battleship, the *Queen Elizabeth*, and Captain Martellotta was to deal with the aircraft carrier.

Just before nine o'clock on the night of December 18 the *Scire* nosed her way into position a mile or so north of Alexandria Harbor. Prince Borghese brought her gently up until her conning tower was just out of the water while her decks were awash. The attackers climbed out of the conning tower and after considerable difficulty managed to pull their chariots from the protecting cylinders. They took their seats and waited as the *Scire* gradually submerged. The launching of the chariots went without a hitch. They were safely afloat.

The sea was flat calm as Lieutenant de la Penne took a look around to get his bearings. The conditions for their attack were as perfect as they could wish for. It was so dark that nothing was visible. Fixing his course, the leader set off with his tiny flotilla towards the harbor entrance. The men were submerged up to the neck, ready to drop under in a moment to avoid being seen. They glided along quietly at about two miles an hour and made such progress that their leader was afraid of arriving before the time scheduled, so they halted awhile to eat some of their rations before they went in to the attack.

They were moving along parallel to the breakwater some distance from the shore when they received a nasty jolt. A motor launch without lights began to speed up and down outside the entrance to the harbor throwing depth charges from time to time to kill any submarine that happened to be lurking thereabouts. They did not like it at all. They sat there with the sea up to their necks, watching the launch that menaced their lives.

But luck was with them. After a while the buoys marking the channel into the harbor lit up. They knew it portended a ship entering or leaving the harbor. Then the lights on the boom itself shone out in the darkness to indicate that the boom across the entrance was to be opened to give passage to a ship.

Here was a heaven-sent opportunity which de la Penne seized avidly. Giving the other crews instructions to dodge into the harbor while the boom was open for the ship, he lurked with them at the harbor mouth awaiting a chance to slip through. Suddenly a destroyer loomed up out of the blackness with another following at a safe interval. The three chariots, going ahead for all they were worth, made for the entrance and managed to steal in undetected in the wake of the warships. It was a perilous passage. The wash flung them about and bumped them against the boom. More than once they were almost capsized by the swell and had difficulty in righting their craft; but they got through safely, the boom closed behind them and the lighted buoys went out, leaving them in absolute darkness to separate and find their way to their targets.

As de la Penne crept into the harbor he detected two cruisers at anchor and recognized the silhouette of the interned French battleship *Lorraine* before he made out the

British battleship that was his target. Moving stealthily towards her, he suddenly hit a steel protection net some fifty or sixty yards away from the hull. It was unexpected. He nosed around seeking a gap like a terrier looking for a rat hole. Taking the chariot down, he hoped to find a way under, but the net touched bottom and he could not get through. His suit was letting in water. He began to feel very cold and wondered how much longer he would be able to carry on.

Surfacing again, he took the risk of manipulating the chariot over the top of the net, fearing all the time that the guns would open up. But he remained unseen, so he moved forward a few yards and then submerged to bring the chariot up to the battleship.

To his chagrin, the chariot stopped dead. A wire had fouled the propellor. Giving his companion Bianci instructions to clear the obstruction, he waited for him to do so. When he went to see if the propeller were freed, he could find no trace of his teammate. Bianci had vanished. Swimming around under the water, de la Penne strove to find the lost mechanic. He was not there. Striking upward to the surface, he swam quietly about seeking him, but Bianci had disappeared.

Wet and cold and rather shaken, he dived again to his chariot and fought to unwind the wire rope which was twisted round the propeller. He struggled and wrenched and strained at it, but it was twisted so tightly that he failed to untangle it.

Being only fifty or sixty feet away from the battleship, he relinquished his efforts to free the propeller and determined to try to move the warhead to the battleship singlehanded. It was a tremendous task that would have been hopeless had the warhead not been slightly buoyant.

The leak in his suit became worse as he dragged the charge slowly along the muddy bottom towards the ship. His exertions were tiring him. His goggles became so misty with sweat that he could not see what he was about. Trying to clear them, he accidently let in a little water and was forced to gulp it down to get rid of it. Rising to the surface to make sure that he had dragged the charge right under the battleship, he went down again to set the time fuse. The task of clipping the charge to the bilge keel was beyond his strength, so he left it lying on the bottom.

Utterly exhausted, he rose to the surface. Tearing the diving gear from his head and back, he started to swim slowly away from the *Valiant*. At once a sentry located the swimmer with an Aldis lamp and raised the alarm. Seachlights flashed out. Machine guns began to chatter. Turning under the bow of the warship, the tired Italian clambered up on a buoy where, to his amazement, he found the missing Bianci.

Losing consciousness in trying to free the propeller, Bianci had floated to the surface where he came to and took refuge on the buoy.

By now the harbor was alive with searchlights. Angry voices shouted from the deck of the battleship as one of the Italians tried to climb a cable. A shot drove him down again and in a few minutes a launch arrived to take the two prisoners to the battleship.

They disclosed that they were Italians, removed their diving suits and handed over their identification papers. News of the capture was passed at once to the *Queen Elizabeth* with a request for an interpreter. Plying the prisoners with questions, the interpreter did his best to get some information from them, but he failed. Then the prisoners were rushed ashore to the Ras-el-Tin naval barracks for another interrogation. This time they were questioned separately by the Chief Intelligence Officer, but not a word would they say about where the charge was placed. Again and again they were pressed to speak, but they steadfastly refused to give anything away.

The presence of the prisoners was proof that dire peril threatened. They were accordingly rushed back to the *Valiant* where her commander, Captain Charles Morgan, again strove to learn the truth from them. They would not speak.

Carrying out the instructions of the Chief Intelligence Officer, Captain Morgan motioned to the Italian officer and told the interpreter to explain that he would be involved in anything that happened to the ship. The prisoner remained silent.

"Take him below," said Captain Morgan.

The prisoner was thereupon escorted to a small compartment deep in the bowels of the ship right over the spot where he had placed the charge. Giving him a glass of rum to warm him up after his long immersion, the British naval officer locked the door on him, leaving him to face the risk of being blown up by his own explosion or of disclosing where the charge was laid.

Meanwhile Engineer Captain Marceglia had managed to identify the silhouette of the battleship that was marked as his quarry. Proceeding quietly toward his target, he bumped into the defense net exactly as de la Penne had done and found that he could not go on. Those defense nets had been placed in position by the special order of Admiral Cunningham only the previous day. It looked as though the British Intelligence service had gained an inkling of what was afoot.

Backing away from the net, Marcegila began to hunt for a way in. Slowly he moved around the barrier, examining it carefully to find a place where he could get through. The net was far too heavy to lift at the bottom to allow him to squeeze underneath. Eventually after scouting around he found a small space that was just big enough to allow the chariot to enter.

No sound came from the *Queen Elizabeth*. Approaching quietly, he took the chariot to the bottom and moved forward until he seemed to be right under the ship. Determined not to make a mistake, he rose to the surface to ensure that he was in the right position, then dived again and began to help his teammate Schergat attach the charge to the bilge keel by the clips. The mechanic who had been breathing oxygen for some time began to suffer the ill-effects. Shaken by severe spasms and feeling very sick, owing to the excess of oxygen, he was forced to abandon his efforts and rest awhile. Marceglia carried on without hesitation and succeeded in attaching the charge and fixing the fuse.

As quietly as they had entered, they stole out of the harbor and made for the beach at Macello, which was very isolated and quiet. They then destroyed all their equipment and wandered ashore to pose as harmless Frenchmen.

Despite the care with which everything had been worked out, the Italian planners made one mistake. They furnished the charioteers with English money which the Egyptians would not accept. The Italians were therefore landed in an enemy country without money or means of sustenance. However, they played their parts astonishingly well all day and after several narrow escapes they made their way to Rosetta.

Their freedom was short-lived. A suspicious Egyptian policeman challenged them on the evening of December 20 and, taking them to Alexandria, handed them over to the British naval authorities.

Captain Martellotta, on the third chariot, was in rather a quandary when he came to look for the aircraft carrier. In spite of a careful search, he failed to locate her. She had in fact already departed from Alexandria. Concluding that she had gone, he began to look for another worth-while target. At first he decided to attack a warship which he thought was a battleship, but recognizing her as a cruiser he drew away. Finally he came on a tanker which he planned to destroy and thereby turn the harbor into a blazing inferno. He aimed to blow up the tanker so that her oil would float out over the surface and then set this oil alight with floating incendiary bombs.

At the critical moment, just as he maneuvered the chariot under the tanker, he, too, fell ill owing to an excess of oxygen. Swimming to the surface, he took off his mask to fill his lungs with fresh air. While he was recovering, his mechanic Marino succeeded in fixing the charge unaided and set the fuse. He then steered the chariot to the surface where Martellotta remounted and they glided away from the tanker and put down four floating incendiary bombs about a hundred yards from the tanker. Jettisoning their equipment, they swam ashore, to enjoy no more than an hour or two of freedom before an Egyptian policeman captured them and handed them to the British authorities.

While these events were happening, de la Penne was immured in the bowels of the *Valiant*. Bianci in another compartment was so worn out with his experiences that he fell fast asleep.

For nearly an hour de la Penne suffered the ordeal, looking anxiously at his watch, wondering if the charge would go off before time or if it would fail. Just before 6 A.M. he could stand the suspense no longer. He hammered on the door and shouted that he wanted to speak to the captain. The master-at-arms ran into the wardroom to tell the captain.

"Bring him up," ordered Captain Morgan.

In a few moments de la Penne appeared before him. "There will soon be an explosion," said the prisoner to the interpreter.

"Where have you put the charge?" the captain demanded.

The prisoner refused to answer.

At that moment came the sound of an explosion from the tanker some distance away. "Is that the explosion?" the captain demanded, through the interpreter.

The prisoner hunched his shoulders.

"Will the *Valiant* be concerned?" they demanded, but de la Penne would give no information.

"Take him down again," ordered the captain.

By now a line had been passed right under the keel of the ship from stem to stern to dislodge any charge that might have been fixed there. As the charge was lying on the sea bed, it was not swept clear. All the watertight doors were closed and the entire crew drawn up on the upper deck where they were told what had happened.

At 6:05 A.M. the *Valiant* heaved under the shock of the explosion. A cataract of water shot up into the heavens and rained down on them as the battleship settled down on the mud.

Lieutenant de la Penne thought the end had come. The floor moved up under his feet, fittings fell about him, the place was filled with acrid smoke. By a miracle he was unharmed except for a slight bruise on the leg. Opening a scuttle, he strove to climb out, but the aperture was too small. Then he tried the entrance. The door opened at his touch and he made his way to the upper deck.

A quarter of a mile away the *Queen Elizabeth* lay at anchor. Even as he gazed across at her in the morning light a great explosion shook her and she, too, settled down in the mud five minutes after the *Valiant*.

Thus two of the finest British battleships were sunk. It was a stunning disaster for the Royal Navy. Its strength had been sadly sapped in evacuating the troops from Greece and Crete. The *Barham* had already been torpedoed with a heavy death roll. The *Warspite* had been knocked out by a bomb which dropped straight down the funnel and ruined the machinery. Now this tragic loss made the Italians masters of the Mediterranean. They could go anywhere they liked and do anything they wanted. Great Britain had not a single battleship in the Mediterranean.

That incredible luck which enabled six men to sink two battleships and a tanker in Alexandria Harbor without the loss of a single life deserted the enemy at the crucial moment. Early on that morning of December 19 Prince Borghese surfaced in the *Scire* off Alexandria and watched anxiously for signs of explosions that would tell him whether the great plan had succeeded. Time passed. Nothing happened. At last unable to risk his ship on the surface any longer, he was compelled to dive and speed away before the explosions occurred.

Five days later, on Christmas Eve, the submarine's captain

waited quietly off Rosetta, scanning the sea and shore in vain for the men who did not come. Returning to the rendezvous on December 26, he watched tensely for the signals that would tell him all was well. There were no signals, no trace of his compatriots, so he was forced to go back without the slightest knowledge of what had happened.

The Italians had achieved one of the most remarkable victories in naval warfare, but they did not know it. That the British were able to keep it dark was as extraordinary as the Italian victory itself. Thousands of British seamen on the sunken battleships knew what had occurred. Axis spies abounded in Cairo and Alexandria. It was phenomenal that nothing leaked out to the enemy. The mass silence of the British sailors was a fine tribute to their discipline and a finer tribute to their patriotism.

The enemy was naturally on tenterhooks to learn the result of the attack. Italian aircraft reconnoitred Alexandria Harbor. Everything looked the same as before. There were no overturned ships, no signs of wreckage. The *Queen Elizabeth* and the *Valiant* rode serenely at their anchors. They were apparently undamaged. The fact that they had sunk and were sitting upright on the bottom was not visible from the air, so the Italians were absolutely deceived and kept their warships safely in harbor instead of exploiting their incredible victory.

On that morning of December 19, 1941, the balance of power in the Mediterranean was dramatically changed. As long as the enemy could be bluffed into believing that British naval power was unaffected, the bitter penalties of disaster might yet be avoided.

Directly the two battleships settled on the mud, the naval command began to grapple with the two most urgent problems — to maintain secrecy and to refloat the ships. The sound of explosions in Alexandria was not unusual. Raiders often flew over to drop bombs, the guns were continually speaking. To casual eyes everything in the harbor seemed to be normal, yet behind the calm exterior all the human resources of the navy suddenly erupted into activity. The first essential was to discover the damage in order to see how it could be rectified.

Calling Commander G. J. Wheeler, Admiral Sir Andrew Cunningham indicated the steps he proposed to take to deal with the *Queen Elizabeth*, and asked for the salvage officer's opinion. The measures suggested would have brought the rescue ships clustering round the battleship like flies round a honeypot.

"Well, sir, they are bound to send a plane over to see what has happened. If they see her with a lot of craft round her they will know they have got her. I suggest that we first of all pump out the oil to bring her upright. If they see her with an oiler alongside there is nothing unusual in that and they will think she is all right," said the Fleet Salvage Officer, and the admiral agreed.

Then the salvage officer got busy on the job, aided by every officer and man on the ships. Naval divers, inspecting the *Valiant*, reported a vast hole in the hull on the port side of the bow between the gun turrets. Without going too closely into details, suffice to say that the hole was large enough to park a bus and still leave room to spare. The flooding of the compartments pulled the bow down and greatly increased the draft forward, which made it necessary to remove as much weight as possible.

A tanker was soon brought alongside and the ship's pumps began to pump out oil. Salvage pumps were brought in to pump out damaged compartments where fractured bulkheads were sealed with pads and shored up. Luckily the light and power plants functioned normally and did all that was asked of them. A steady stream of oil gushed from the *Valiant* into the tanker while the salvage pumps sucked the water out of the bowels of the ship. Gradually her slight list was corrected and she came upright. Thousands of tons of water and oil were pumped out. Prudence, however, dictated that the water flooding the depth charges should remain undisturbed. Anchors, cables, shells, and charges were lifted out of the ship as fast as men could work.

Before midday on December 20, 1941, the *Valiant* was ready to float over the keel blocks in the dry dock with eight or nine inches to spare. But the salvage officer was not satisfied. Work continued for the rest of the day, removing ammunition and other things until the bow of the ship was raised another six or seven inches. Then at nine o'clock on the morning of December 21, just fifty-one hours after she was sunk, the *Valiant* was maneuvered safely into dry dock to be repaired. It was a magnificent feat, due, as the Fleet Salvage Officer said, to the splendid co-operation of all the officers and men aboard.

Sitting on the mud with a slight list, the *Queen Elizabeth* was not so easy to deal with. Robbed of light and power by the explosion, she was wrapped in gloom until submarines could be brought up to supply these necessaries. Then the naval divers, working in the mud and feeling their way under the hull, were very baffled. That there must be a hole was obvious, otherwise the battleship would not be resting on the sea bed. Yet although they explored the bottom foot by foot for hour after hour they could not find it. Terribly handicapped by the ooze, they had to work by touch, for despite the care with which they moved they could not avoid fogging the water. On a clean, sandy bottom they could have seen perfectly by the light of the sun; but the mud on the bottom combined with the gloom caused by the overhang of the ship, which cut off the light, forced them to work blind.

All through the morning and afternoon the search for the damage was pursued. It was not until seven o'clock in the evening, thirteen hours after the explosion, that the divers were able to locate an opening in the ship's hull. It was more of a fissure than a hole, seven or eight feet long by a couple of inches wide. It puzzled the salvage officer how so small an opening could achieve such big results.

Next day the divers went down to continue their examination, but in their all-day search they failed to find the hole which they had examined overnight. This gives an idea of the difficulties under which they worked. Darkness had fallen before they came upon a clamp attached to the bilge of the ship. The line hanging from the clamp told them that the charge must have been fixed in the vicinity.

Meanwhile the pumps transferred hundreds of tons of fuel oil from the *Queen Elizabeth* to the tanker. The men worked ceaselessly to remove the ammunition to lighten the ship. Flooded boiler rooms indicated that the damage was in that neighborhood, although the divers could not find it. Long experience had taught Commander Wheeler that there must be broken inlets which would cause a deal of trouble if they were overlooked, so he ordered plugs and pads to be prepared to seal them while the task of shoring up weakened bulkheads went on inside the ship.

Three days after the explosion the battleship was brought into an upright position. The large weight of oil and ammunition discharged had reduced her draft by eight or nine inches. It seemed little enough after all their efforts, yet to the salvage officer the gain was appreciable.

Even now the extent of the damage remained unknown. There was not the slightest sign on deck that anything had happened. Nothing was broken or displaced. It was an astonishing state of affairs that mystified the salvage officer. As a rule a ship's deck will give some indication of where the damage is situated below. But the upperworks of the *Queen Elizabeth* gave nothing away.

With the naval divers working until exhausted, it became obvious that more were required to cope with the work to be done, yet not another diver was available on the station. The decision was now made to use compressed air to drive the water from some of the flooded compartments to regain buoyancy. By the night of December 23 the bow of the *Queen Elizabeth* was raised another three or four inches.

On Christmas Eve a gale kept the divers from working until late in the afternoon, but when they went down at last they were able for the first time to gain something like a true idea of the damage. There was a hole under the boiler room that would have engulfed a couple of suburban houses. As the ship had been sitting on it, the divers were unable to find it until she began to rise. The divers spent Christmas Day checking and confirming the damage.

Now that the worst was known, the help of other divers became imperative. In this emergency Admiral Cunningham dispatched a request for divers to the Commander in Chief of the South Atlantic Fleet, Rear Admiral D. A. Burgen at Simonstown in South Africa, and on December 26 Lieutenant Keeble started to fly from Cairo to Cape Town in his quest for divers to salve the *Queen Elizabeth*.

The South African Minister of Railways came to the rescue with the offer of four divers, Priestly, Davidson, Shorrt, and Winter who were on the staff of the railways. Satisfying himself that they were capable of doing the work required, Lieutenant Keeble asked them if they would volunteer for a special job which was very important and very secret.

"You will be away some weeks," he told them.

All agreed instantly. Knowing nothing, the only thing they could tell their families was not to expect them back too soon. When they started out for Pretoria on January 17, 1942, their ultimate destination was a profound secret. Reaching Zwartkop on January 19, they embarked in an aircraft, still puzzling over their destination. Landing at last in Cairo they were rushed to Alexandria by car to meet Commander Wheeler, who explained what he wanted them to do.

The Fleet Salvage Officer and his team had not been idle. They had wrestled to get recalcitrant salvage pumps to the spots where they could suck the water out of flooded compartments. They had heaved out the giant anchors and mighty cables. They had fitted connection after connection in readiness for the air compressors.

The work was never-ending, and all their toil seemed to make little change. Yet the difference, almost imperceptible, was eagerly marked by the salvage officer. His careful measurements showed that the bow was slowly swinging up, not much, it is true, half an inch, an inch, or two inches. Every ton taken out gave the battleship a little extra buoyancy. From forty-two feet which marked the draft at the bow after the explosion, the salvage squads had managed by December 28, 1941, to reduce it to thirty-nine feet two inches.

Commander Wheeler was under no illusion. Before he could move the ship into dry dock he had to reduce her draft to something under thirty-five feet. He was six inches on the right side aft, but over four feet to the bad forward.

A diver on loan from the Suez Canal Company sought to explore through the mighty hole in the double bottom of the ship. The jagged edges of torn and twisted plates made his movements hazardous. An air pipe caught and cut by the sharp spurs of metal, a tear in his diving suit might have proved fatal. Moving warily in the blackness, he penetrated upward for fifteen feet in an effort to find the boilers. Thwarted in his efforts to locate them, in spite of their immense size, he made his way down again and emerged safely.

That day of December 30, 1941, the compressed-air connections on which the salvage officer set high hopes were completed, and next day the compressors started to pump air into the compartments adjoining the boiler room to try to gain that much-needed extra buoyancy. New Year's Day passed to the steady rhythm of the air compressors, but the ship gave no sign of responding. The next day, and the next, the air compressors worked ceaselessly to force the water out, with little effect.

The failure of the compressed air to produce the expected results led the salvage officer to try out the four pumps that had been introduced into the boiler room. They might have been pumping in the open sea for all the impression they made. The puzzling thing was that the divers could not find where the water was coming in. Eventually some days later they detected it flowing into the boiler room against one of the bulkheads, but a chaos of twisted metal prevented them from tracing where it came from.

An urgent message from the Fleet Salvage Officer brought a prompt response from the manager of the Liverpool and Glasgow Salvage Association who rushed out a first-class diver, Peter Taylor, by air to Cairo to assist on the *Queen Elizabeth*. At this juncture the four divers arrived from South Africa. Never were divers more sadly needed nor gladly welcomed. Working on the diving stage in inky darkness under the guidance of Peter Taylor, they began to burn a way through the ship's bottom, carving away masses of jagged plates with their underwater cutters.

These cutters, so commonplace to divers, are nevertheless a remarkable example of the inventive powers of man. That a flame can be kept alight in the depths of the sea remains something of a miracle. There are two main types of underwater cutters, electric and gas. Both can burn their way through steel plates that are completely immersed in water. The electric cutters form their earth with the plate itself and develop a terrific temperature of about 2000 degrees centigrade. In the gas cutters used on the *Queen Elizabeth* the flame was forced out at high pressure through a blowpipe, thus driving the water away from the immediate vicinity of the nozzle and enabling the flame to melt through the metal. Needless to add, the correct operation of these cutters demanded much experience and skill on the part of the divers.

Their work was complicated by the presence of fuel oil which compelled them to use their blowpipes with great care

to avoid starting a raging fire with results that might easily
have spelled disaster for the divers on the job. They drove
ahead for a dozen hours a day until they were ready to drop.
When they came to the surface, their attendants stripped off
their diving suits and set them out to dry, while the divers
went off to enjoy an hour's relaxation before turning in to
sleep till dawn. Then came the usual routine of donning their
diving suits and slipping down to the stages to resume their
fight to save the *Queen Elizabeth*.

By January 28, 1942, they had successfully cut their way
through the inner bottom and were able to explore the flooded
boiler room which had defied the battery of pumps. The
reason was clear. The entire steel floor had been blown away,
but by some extraordinary fluke the fittings and machinery
had escaped damage.

For three days they made desperate efforts to carry out
temporary repairs to enable the boiler room to be cleared of
water. Unfortunately the damage was too severe to be sur-
mounted under the prevailing conditions, so the salvage officer
was obliged to suspend operations.

Now that she was afloat once more, the *Queen Elizabeth*
was moved out to moorings in the harbor on February 1.
Within a few days a full-scale test with air compressors and
pumps proved that she could pass into the dock as soon as it
was ready to receive her.

Throughout the Italians remained unaware of their astounding success. The men in the chariots had been swallowed up in
the night and had vanished without trace, while the guns of
the *Queen Elizabeth* stuck out menacingly from their turrets
as a symbol of the might of the Royal Navy.

Perhaps a musical comedy performed on board the battleship for three days did much to mislead the enemy. Whether
it was part of a big bluff may be hotly denied in naval circles
where they argue that you cannot throw thousands of sailors

out of work without giving them something to amuse them. Anyway, it was a good show for which many invitations were sent out to the notabilities of Cairo and Alexandria as well as farther afield to Arab dignitaries and sheiks.

The ship rang with applause as the comedians cracked their jokes and sang their songs. The navy excelled itself. The guests were delighted. They remained in utter ignorance of the fact that the battleship was floating on compressed air. That performance on the *Queen Elizabeth* was a phenomenal success. It was the talk of Alexandria for days. By the time whispers of it reached Italy it had somehow become transformed into a diplomatic reception, which convinced the enemy that there was nothing wrong with the *Queen Elizabeth*. The press conferences which the Admiral held on board may also have done much to confirm that the ship was all right.

Thus the astounding luck of the attackers was neutralized by the amazing luck of the defenders. That six men could accomplish so much and so many men could keep it secret are alike unbelievable.

On April 5, 1942, the *Queen Elizabeth* went into dry dock at Alexandria. At the same time the *Valiant* was passing through the Suez Canal on her way to Simonstown for permanent repairs. Some months later the *Queen Elizabeth* also passed through the Canal on her way to the United States where she was made battleworthy once more.

There was a strange sequel to the sinking of the *Valiant*. In 1944, after the Allies had defeated Italy, Captain Charles Morgan of the *Valiant* was appointed Rear Admiral Commanding the Naval Base at Taranto. One day de la Penne, who had returned from the prisoner of war camp in India, met the English naval officer whose ship he had sunk in Alexandria Harbor. "I couldn't answer your questions when you pressed me in 1941, because I hadn't been able to make fast the charge to your ship's keel. It was only resting on the bottom, and if you had known that, you could have escaped damage by simply going ahead for a short distance," explained de la Penne.

At a later date the Italian chariot expert fought on the side of the Allies and made a brilliant attack on the German ships in the harbor of Spezia. This led Admiral Morgan to recommend his old enemy for a British decoration. As the two countries were still theoretically at war with each other, this decoration could not be granted.

At Taranto in March 1945, however, Prince Umberto of Italy, accompanied by Admiral Morgan, was awarding decorations won in the war by Italian naval officers and men, when he came to Lieutenant Luigi de la Penne who had won the Medaglia d'Oro al Valor Militare for his successful attack in Alexandria Harbor. "I think this is your turn," said Prince Umberto to Admiral Morgan.

With a smile, Admiral Morgan took the gold medal from its case and pinned it upon the breast of the man who had sunk his ship.

CHAPTER IV

Captain Hamilton's Triumph

As Captain F. S. Hamilton cast a backward glance from the bridge of the steamship *Hororata* and saw Liverpool receding in the distance, his mind was too occupied with his chances of escaping the U-boats in the Atlantic to wonder whether number 13 was lucky or unlucky. Maybe he was not superstitious. But whether all the members of the crew were indifferent to the fact that they were starting their voyage to Wellington, New Zealand, on September 13, 1941, they alone could tell.

A fine new ship, the *Hororata* had recently been added to the fleet of the New Zealand Shipping Line. She was big, 12,090 tons gross, she was fast with a designed speed of sixteen knots, so it was safer for her to sail alone than in convoy and rely upon her speed to save her from enemy submarines. Her maiden voyage had pleased captain and crew and owners. Her engines had settled down, and her captain knew just how she would behave in calm and storm.

With her lookouts scanning the seas for the sight of periscopes, she began her voyage by speeding southwestward for nearly five thousand miles across the Atlantic hunting grounds of the U-boats, to crawl through the Panama Canal. Then she picked up speed again to continue her southwesterly course across the Pacific for between six and seven thousand miles to Wellington, where she arrived on October 16, 1942. It was a fast trip.

Unloading her munitions, she moved northward along the coast of North Island to Auckland, where the dockside derricks dropped much cargo into her refrigerated holds. Then she turned southward to Canterbury to take in the cargo waiting for her at Lyttleton, and by the time it was stowed she was packed with thousands of tons of butter and meat and cheese, earmarked as rations for the British people, not to mention thousands of bales of wool and much hemp and lead to feed British factories.

As she cast off, her captain rang down for slow ahead to take her out of that wonderful harbor, then he headed northeast for Bilbao. Her chief engineer Mr. A. A. McGregor was a proud man during that long run to Panama, for her engines, designed for sixteen knots, logged a steady seventeen.

Moving sedately through the locks of the Panama Canal, she quickened her pace again as she dropped the West Indies astern to speed through the mysterious Sargasso Sea and face the U-boat packs that were hunting anything afloat.

Rough weather slowed her down when she needed all the speed she possessed. She pushed on through the Sargasso Sea day after day while her lookouts continued to gaze around on the heaving seas for a sight of the dreaded periscope. As she was thrashing along, and altering course according to plan, the treacherous Japanese aircraft dropped out of the skies at Pearl Harbor to deal their shattering blow at the United States Navy, bringing Japan in with the Axis to share out, as she thought, the spoils of war. Meanwhile dozens of U-boats were hunting in the Atlantic, relying upon their secret information to intercept British convoys, and paying special attention to the area round the Azores.

It may be recalled that on December 12, 1941, the Japanese aircraft struck again; this time it was a blow at the Royal Navy, for they sank the new battleship *Prince of Wales* as well as the *Repulse* in Malayan waters. This shook Mr. Churchill, whose friend Admiral Tom Phillips was drowned. But the man to whom the civilized world owes so much wrote in *Their Finest Hour:* "The only thing that ever really frightened me during the war was the U-boat peril."

That was indeed the greatest peril of all. No master of a ship knew when the invisible enemy would strike.

The next day it came on to blow harder than ever from the northwest. The gale whipped the tops off the great seas that hammered away at the *Hororata* until she was compelled to slow down to eleven knots. Changing course from time to time, she drove ahead towards the Azores.

About three-thirty in the afternoon a lurking U-boat got her. There was a dull boom as a cascade of water shot up from her port side. She rolled in her gait and began to spill boxes of butter into the sea through a big gap in No. 4 and No. 5 holds. As the sea washed in, she heeled to port under the weight of water which slowly pulled down her stern.

The German who fired the torpedo was convinced that it was his lucky day. He saw the torpedo running true, watched the explosion, peered eagerly through the periscope as the fine ship heeled under the blow. In his eyes the *Hororata* was doomed, and he proudly announced his kill to the German Naval Command.

Captain Hamilton, with more prudence, refused to jump to any such conclusion. Seeing that the ship was hit on the port side, he rang down to reduce the speed of the other engine and swung her stern on to reduce the target if the enemy attacked again. Automatically the crew ran to their stations. There was not a single casualty.

While the chief officer, Mr. R. W. Coen, went to take soundings to get some idea of the damage, the chief engineer made a quick examination of the engine room. Everything was in order. The U-boat commander had made a trifling miscalculation, a mere second or two, but long enough to carry the engine room past the approaching torpedo and leave the two refrigerated holds to take the impact of the explosion.

Whether it had saved the *Hororata* from disaster, Captain Hamilton did not know. The engineer reassured him that everything in the engine room was intact and he could give any speed that was called for. The ship had answered her helm perfectly when she swung stern on to the attacker, so she was under control. Two holds were flooded. The seas were playing havoc with the boxes of butter that went bobbing away in the wake of the vessel. She had a nasty list and was sinking by the stern.

The nearest island in the Azores was over two hundred miles away. Whether the captain could reach safety or not was problematical. Even with two holds flooded he might keep her afloat if he could balance her and give her a little more buoyancy astern. Accordingly he gave orders to discharge the fresh water in the after tank over the side. It lightened the stern considerably. Then the fuel oil was pumped out of the tank under the flooded No. 5 hold into an empty tank forward, to add still further to the margin of safety.

Now the gale which had slowed her down to make a presentable target for the U-boat began to abate. With the coming of darkness the winds and seas both eased off. The captain pushed her along as fast as he dared. All the time the stern was sinking in the water. Throughout that night with all its anxieties he nursed his ship along and by dawn was within sight of safety.

Her engines were reduced to dead slow. She was listing so badly that it looked as though she was about to overturn. Any use of the rudder aggravated this tendency. The decks were canting at a nasty angle. The loss of cargo had made her unstable. In the last hour or two it was definitely touch-and-go, but Captain Hamilton succeeded in bringing his ship with her full complement of eighty-two officers and crew safely to anchor in Vera Cruz Bay.

She was in such a dangerous condition that he ordered most of the crew ashore to ensure their safety if she overturned.

There was little shelter where she lay. The local port captain warned Captain Hamilton that bad weather was on the way and if a gale blew up in the night there was no prospect of anyone getting off the ship or landing ashore, for the cliffs were too steep.

In the circumstances the captain and his remaining officers went ashore. All night the *Hororata* tugged viciously at her anchors as the gale hit her. All night the captain and his chief officer and chief engineer watched her anxiously from the shore, wondering if her anchors would hold or whether she would capsize in a squall. While they watched they discussed the possibilities of increasing her stability and concluded that their only chance was to fill No. 3 fuel tank with 500 tons of fuel oil. Stricken as she was, the *Hororata* was not yet lost.

As early as possible the captain took his chief officer and engineers and half a dozen seamen back to the ship. Steam was raised, and the engineers succeeded in transferring the 500 tons of oil to the tank where the weight would do much to correct the list of the ship. It was one step to safety. Meanwhile they saw that the refrigerating machinery was keeping the other holds at the right temperature to preserve the cargo.

That night, with a skeleton crew on board, the ship dragged her anchors during a gale and drifted twenty miles along the coast. It took them two hours to steam back. When they arrived, they found that four of their lifeboats which were grounded ashore had been smashed by the breakers.

To allow the *Hororata* to remain in that exposed position was to invite disaster. The captain and officers realized that they must get the ship to a more sheltered spot if they wished to keep her afloat. The nearest port was Horta in Fayal island 150 miles away. Leaving the majority of the crew ashore, where the local authorities had kindly provided them with accommodations in the hospital, the captain sailed with his skeleton crew. There was just room for them all in the two remaining boats if she foundered on the way. To avoid the risk of meeting another U-boat, the captain prudently left after dark without advising anyone of his intentions, so that any spy snooping around would not be able to pass on the news.

They logged a steady twelve knots all night, to steam safely through Fayal Strait and drop anchor in the outer harbor of Horta just before eight o'clock next morning, December 18. Still too exposed to the weather, she was so down by the stern that it was doubtful if she could be taken into the inner harbor. However, Captain Antonio Bello, the port captain, and the chief pilot managed with considerable difficulty to maneuver her in beside the mole. This gave her shelter for the greater part of her length, though she remained exposed for about 150 feet.

Not until she was safely anchored and moored did Captain Hamilton begin to breathe freely. With indomitable courage he had managed to keep his ship afloat. Now he was determined, if it was humanly possible, to take her with her invaluable cargo back to England. That meant repairs. And repairs involved many problems.

In the old days of the sailing ship he could have run his vessel ashore on a sandy beach and careened her to make repairs and caulk her planks, as Drake did when he first sailed round the world. With a modern ship big enough to carry a fleet of Golden Hinds it was impossible to run her ashore without risking disaster, and the mere idea of careening her to get at her damage was ludicrous.

The modern method to replace the easy ways of the old days was to move the ship into dry dock. Unhappily there was no dry dock available in Horta and consequently Captain Hamilton and Captain Bello, along with the chief pilot and harbor engineer, all pooled their ideas to see how they could manage without one. Meanwhile they set to work to improve the stability of the ship. Knowing that the best way to get at the damage was to lighten her, they enlisted the aid of the local Portuguese dockers who were soon unloading cargo and taking it ashore for temporary storage. The refrigerators were kept running in the undamaged holds to preserve the perishables.

The work of the dockers was not always enviable. Bad meat in one of the holds raised such a stench that it was intolerable, yet the men managed to endure it until they had loaded the rotten meat into lighters and dumped it out at sea. The removal of cargo aft brought up the ship's stern to disclose some of the damage she had suffered, though the major portion remained hidden under water. When the local diver at length finished his survey he found a hole twenty-three feet long and twenty-one feet deep.

The work went on day after day, removing the cargo, probing round to find what other damage had been done. On Christmas Eve a smaller hole was discovered a little farther along the hull. It added to their troubles. The only way to make her seaworthy was to patch her. And the only way they could patch her was with timber.

The Portuguese are Great Britain's oldest allies. Although the Portuguese authorities in Horta possessed such meager facilities for so huge a task, they lacked neither enthusiasm nor imagination. Nothing like the patching of the *Hororata* had ever been attempted before in Horta. Captain Bello, who took charge of the work, hunted round for suitable timber to build a patch. There was none available. This setback would have wrecked the hopes of most men, but the little group of enthusiasts in Horta were not easily discouraged.

If there was no timber, were there no trees growing on the hillsides? There were, pine trees in abundance. Collecting the local laborers, Captain Bello accompanied them up into the hills with Captain Hamilton to fell trees. Suitable trees were marked and the men went to work to cut them down. As one tree after another toppled to the ground, the top growth was cleared and the trunks were hitched to oxen and dragged down to the local sawmill where the circular saw shrilled loudly as it cut the trees into planks eight inches wide by four inches thick.

Salvage men are geniuses at make-do-and-mend, but never in my long experience of marine salvage have I known them to cut down living trees and saw them into planks to make the patch which saved their ship. This is the spirit that will accomplish anything.

Even when the hull presents a flat surface, fitting a patch is very troublesome. When the plates have ragged edges that are distorted by an explosion the difficulties are magnified. Along the bottom edge of the gap in the *Hororata* was a long line of rivet holes where the rivets had been driven out by the torpedo. These holes were a great advantage to the salvors, for they made use of them to save the immense labor of drilling holes by hand in the old-fashioned way. Rivet holes in the top edges of the plates were also brought into use. The task of covering the hole with vertical planks went slowly forward. To insure that the planks fitted snugly over the distortions in the plates, the divers molded sections of wire into all the irregularities. With these wire templates to guide them, the local workmen chipped away with adzes until the wood was shaped to fit, using with great skill these ancient tools that had not changed since the birth of Christ.

Not only had they to cut down the trees to make the planks, they also had to forge every rivet and bolt used on the work. About halfway up the hole, just above sea level, a strong balk of timber was fitted across the whole length of the damage to make a firm bearing for the middle of the patch. This timber was shored from inside the ship.

Plank by plank the patch was bolted home by the divers undersea and the shipwrights above until the gigantic hole and the smaller hole were covered in. All the joints were carefully caulked and strips of wood were nailed over them where necessary. When finished, the patch was covered over with tarpaulins to give it a waterproof exterior.

Setting the pumps to work in the flooded holds, the salvors slowly reduced the water until they were able to see for the first time what the torpedo had done to the hull. The damage actually extended to a length of forty-five feet and a depth of thirty-one feet. It was so extensive that Captain Hamilton and his salvage advisers concluded that the wooden patch would have to be backed with a concrete patch inside the hull. Accordingly the carpenters made an enormous wooden box three feet wide to cover the entire area of the damaged hull, and in six days this was filled with 320 tons of concrete to reinforce the wooden patch.

All the time Captain Hamilton and his Portuguese colleagues were handicapped by a lack of suitable materials. They required many strips of steel plate five eighths of an inch thick and from twenty-eight to thirty-two feet long. Some of these were cut with a gas cutter. When the gas ran out the Portuguese artisans did not hesitate to cut the remainder by hand. It was incredibly hard work, but they did it cheerfully.

Seeking shores to strengthen the ship, Captain Bello looked around and could find nothing suitable. Then someone remembered a streetcar line that had been made to convey stone down from the mountains to build Horta cathedral, so the rails of the streetcar line were pulled up and utilized. Still the salvors wanted more steel strips for strengthening. There was no more steel strip in all Horta. There was in the ship, however, a good deal of brine piping which had been damaged by the explosion. The salvors seized on this, cut it into suitable lengths and hammered it flat. It served quite well in the emergency.

Time and again when the salvors were baffled by a shortage of materials, they made use of something else. They refused to be beaten.

By March 4, the ship was reloaded and had been granted a seaworthy certificate. She was lying in the inner harbor waiting for her escort when she broke adrift in a full gale which raged on March 13. Thus the cryptic number 13 cropped up once more in her short history, but as she suffered no harm it must be assumed that it was her lucky day.

It was on December 14, that Captain Hamilton had brought her to the Azores in a sinking condition. In three months, with the enthusiastic help of the local authorities and workers he had patched her and pumped her out and restowed her cargo. In view of the primitive facilities and paucity of materials it was a remarkable feat.

On St. Patrick's day, March 17, he sailed after dark, escorted by H.M.S. *Burwell*. Within three days the *Burwell* was in trouble and the lame duck had to assist the destroyer by supplying her with twenty-six tons of diesel oil and forty tons of water — it was no easy job transferring them in the heavy swell.

She arrived back in Liverpool on March 23 with nearly 10,000 tons of cargo intact out of the 11,300 tons of cargo she had stowed in New Zealand.

CHAPTER V

Refloating the Georgic

Packed with cargo, and alive with troops who were destined to build up the strength of the British Army in Egypt for another fight with Rommel, the Cunard liner *Georgic* in command of Captain A. C. Greig moved steadily northward up the Red Sea. The *Georgic* was a ship to be proud of, a fine motor vessel built for comfort as well as speed. She was 684 feet 6 inches long and 27,759 tons gross. At that time when a voyage through the Mediterranean was fraught with such peril from enemy bombers, she played an important part in carrying troops and cargo swiftly round the Cape to Egypt.

Arriving at Port Suez, she disembarked her troops and discharged her cargo. Then she began to take on mails and many passengers who were being evacuated to Cape Town as well as those who were returning to the United Kingdom.

As she lay at anchor in Suez Bay about three o'clock on the afternoon of July 14, 1941, the drone of aircraft was heard and a number of enemy bombers suddenly appeared. The anti-aircraft guns opened up, but the bombers flew on. The *Georgic*, lying immobile below them, was a rich prize. Had she been at sea she might have escaped by taking evasive action. But the enemy caught her lying helplessly at her moorings. A bomb struck the hull on the port side of the ship near No. 4 hold and glanced off to explode under water with a shock that made the liner roll as though she were a rowboat instead of a mighty ship over two hundred yards long. Another bomb aimed with greater accuracy hit the boat deck. Penetrating the promenade deck, it exploded with immense force in No. 5

hold. Splinters from the bomb-casing cut through the bulk-heads, making them leaky. The blast drove through the ship in a wall of fire that set the passenger quarters ablaze and in a short time the smoke was billowing out of the stricken liner and she began to cant as the water poured through the rents in her hull.

Forbidden to run the gantlet of the Mediterranean because of enemy bombers, she had steamed slap into the very danger she had striven to evade. In seeking safety, she had traveled an extra ten thousand miles round Africa, only to fall victim to the bombers in the end.

Her value to the war effort could not be computed. Now she was sinking and in flames and none could tell what the end would be.

The shock of the explosion had barely died away when the captain began to marshal the passengers into the boats and get them ashore. Many of the passengers had the most extraordinary escapes, but a dozen members of the gun crew were killed and several injured.

As soon as the boats were away, Captain Greig sought to save the ship. Hauling up the anchor, he rang down to the engine room for slow ahead and started the burning liner moving toward the shallows at the north of Suez Bay. He soon found that the liner was unmanageable. The steering had been damaged by the explosion.

Crashing against the H.M.S. *Glenearn,* which was moored some distance away, the *Georgic* pushed on implacably, quite out of control, until she thrust her nose hard on a coral reef which held her fast. The water was pouring in aft, flames and smoke were shooting from portholes, she was listing as though about to overturn.

The master had done all that was humanly possible. Ordering up the engineers, who with the officers and crew had stood gallantly at their posts during this ordeal, he followed them into a boat just after four o'clock.

Fifty minutes earlier the *Georgic* was a proud liner. In less than an hour she had become a blazing wreck.

She had many things on board which were wanted in the United Kingdom, yet the most precious did not consist of bullion or gems — it was a captured German tank. This tank was being shipped to England so that experts could make a thorough examination to find out the latest technical developments of the enemy. Carefully guarded, the monster had been brought to Suez and loaded. Now it seemed fated to be destroyed by fire or sunk in the sea.

Half a dozen men were anxious that it should not happen. Realizing how much might depend upon this enemy tank, they were bent on saving it.

"It's madness!" exclaimed those who sought to restrain them.

By then the ship was shot with smoke and flames from end to end. Heavy explosions took place as the fire reached the magazines. From moment to moment further explosions threatened. Conditions were intolerable and the survival of anyone attempting to remove the tank was problematical.

The men were not concerned with the risk. Their thoughts were dominated by the unknown secrets concealed in the captured tank.

Brushing aside warnings, they took a floating crane out to the burning ship and scrambled aboard. She was listing badly. The heat and smoke were stifling. For all they knew, the tank might break away down the tilting deck and charge through the rails into the sea.

Ignoring the dangers and protecting themselves from the heat as best they could, they struggled to get a couple of slings under the tank. Eyebrows and hair were singed, faces grimed with smoke, and feet scorched by the heat of the decks before they succeeded in coaxing the slings into place. Not until they had assured themselves that the slings were secure enough to recover the tank without letting it slip did they give the signal to the floating crane to lift clear. Thus they saved it for the experts in England.

In the third volume of The Second World War Sir Winston Churchill, whose foresight and energy led to the British Army being equipped with tanks in the First World War, tells how he was so apprehensive about British tanks in the Western Desert and the future developments of this vital weapon that, on April 20, 1941, he wrote notes to the Secretary of State for War and the Minister of Supply pointing out that some German tanks had been captured in Libya and asking that an expert should study them immediately and that a tank should be sent home for examination. This German tank which was so gallantly recovered from the burning *Georgic* was probably the tank which Churchill started on its journey from Libya to England.

Throughout that night of July 14 the *Georgic* sent a pillar of fire and smoke into the air as the combustible material was consumed. When Commander Wheeler arrived from Haifa on July 17, three days after the attack, there were still pockets of fire burning in various parts of the ship, and she was giving off such heat and fumes that he was driven off her before he could make a complete examination. He endeavored to find out from the survivors exactly what had happened after the bombing, but accounts were too confused to obtain a complete picture.

For the next two days the fumes and smoke maintained the intolerable conditions. But on July 22, after she had been burning and smoldering for a week, she cleared sufficiently to allow him to go aboard to assess the damage.

It was bad enough, so bad that in normal times the *Georgic* would probably have been written off as a total loss and no attempt made to refloat her. But times were not normal. A war was raging, and there was a consensus of opinion that the liner must be refloated. She was grounded from stem to stern and flooded up to the boat decks from No. 4 hold to right aft.

What damage she had sustained in the hull and down in the holds could be discovered only by a diver. Whatever it was, the salvage officer felt sure he could refloat her, given the necessary material and skilled labor.

In the absence of definite orders, he carried on with many other tasks elsewhere, and it was not until August 30 that diver P. Hansen dropped down the shot rope to make a thorough survey of the liner's hull. The *Georgic* was a big ship, and it took the diver four days to make a rigorous examination. On the starboard side, from the waterline to about ten feet below it, plate after plate was buckled from amidships to the stern. This was due to the bomb which glanced off the hull and exploded in the water. On the port side, from the front of the bridge for a distance of nearly forty feet towards the stern, the four lower rows of plates above the bilge keel were pushed in for about two feet. There was an upright crack two feet long and nearly two inches wide, and a seam gaping open for a dozen feet, while her bow was damaged through colliding with the *Glenearn*.

Twelve days after the diver made his report the order was issued to refloat the *Georgic*. The wires began to hum. The salvage ship *Confederate*, summoned from the Mediterranean, arrived at Suez on the night of September 15. A first-class salvage team of a diver and twelve men were ordered down from Haifa, along with four Greek divers from Alexandria. They wasted no time on the way.

Meanwhile the salvage officer cast round for pumps and got all he could, though not as many as he would have liked, from Alexandria and Port Said. He calculated that when the liner was made tight he would have about 50,000 tons of water to shift from her, with no more than three six-inch motor pumps, a ten-inch motor pump and an eight-inch steam pump to do the job. In the meantime there was the problem of making the liner watertight.

Before that could be started the salvage ship had to get

alongside her. The davits from which the boats had been launched were still outboard, as were the ship's derricks. The ropes trailing in the sea were a deadly snare to any propeller that came into contact with them, so it was necessary to swing in all the davits and derricks to allow the *Confederate* to moor there. Making their way to the boat deck, the salvage men began methodically to pull them all inboard to get the lines out of the way.

The carpenters were soon actively engaged in constructing about 150 patches for the submerged gangway doors and portholes to make them tight for pumping operations. Other men started to rig the wooden stages from which the divers could work. As soon as the stages were in place, the divers began to plug the dozens of inlets and outlets of the engines and lavatories in the sides of the ship.

The men looked like pygmies moving about the liner. It seemed crazy to think that what they were doing could shift the stricken monster. They were so few, about eighteen all told. But there was magic in their touch. Every blow they struck was a blow to restore buoyancy. They were experts working under one of the masters of their craft.

The handicaps under which they toiled would have beaten most men, even if the necessary mechanical power was at their command. But it was not. The *Georgic* was run by electricity. All her auxiliary engines were electric. She could furnish no power at all to help them. Yet without power the salvors could not do the job. There were patches to be raised and lowered, heavy weights to be slung, masses of metal to be cut and moved out of the way to let the men get at some vital point. All these things demanded power which was not available.

Four of the ship's engineers who were familiar with the engines were glad to lend their aid to the salvage party in an effort to obtain power. Casting skillful eyes over the electric winches on deck, the engineers began to test them to see if they were workable. With knowing hands backed by expert knowledge they manipulated the windlass.

"They might go, if we had the juice," they said.

Without it the salvage men were stumped. It was heartening to know that winches and windlass might work; but where the power was coming from to set them turning was a tougher puzzle.

"If we had a portable generator, it would be all right," someone suggested.

The salvage officer nodded in agreement. He began to wonder where a portable generator could be found. Inquiries went round Port Suez and drew a blank. Then a telephone search was made in every corner of the dockyard in Alexandria, without finding what was wanted. The search widened and inquiries filtered through to the likeliest places in Cairo where many failures ultimately led to success, for the persistent salvage officer finally located a generator and had it sent down to Suez.

The generator, however, was but a partial solution of the problem. It could not produce electric current by magic. Like the electric winches, it was a dead and useless thing without the power to work it. Thus with two parts of the problem solved, they were still up against the main problem of power. A portable boiler mocked at them, because the generator was not driven by steam. It was driven by a belt.

Now the hunt began for a self-contained engine that was run by a belt. It was not easy to find, but their inquiries at length led them to unearth a secondhand farm tractor. Thus a farm tractor, by a queer twist of fate, was set up on the deck of the *Georgic* where it was linked with the generator to generate electricity to turn the winches. In this way the salvage officer was able to provide the juice.

With power available, the preparations went ahead at a fine pace. Forward, a section of the bow was removed where it had been damaged in collision with the warship, the plates were bolted together and made tight inside with concrete to give buoyancy to several chambers there. The ticklish job of heaving up the anchor and cable was undertaken by the salvage ship. As the anchor alone weighed ten tons without the cable, it put a big strain on the *Confederate's* gear before it was safely housed.

One thing which irked the salvage officer was the loss of time incurred by the divers during mine-sweeping operations in the port. Every time the sweepers started work, the divers had to knock off. The Royal Air Force, of course, was not alone in making itself a nuisance by mining enemy ports. The Germans, who led the way in this art, were past masters at it. They knew quite well that if they could block the port and stop up the Suez Canal they might be able to hold up the British effort long enough to allow Rommel to get to Cairo. To help their campaign they did their best by dropping mines and bombs at every opportunity. This called for the unremitting attention of the mine sweepers. In the end it was arranged that the mine sweepers should work all night from four o'clock in the afternoon until nine o'clock the following morning, leaving the divers free to work undisturbed from nine o'clock in the morning until four o'clock in the afternoon. This amicable arrangement functioned perfectly, to the satisfaction of all.

One by one the portholes were patched; plugs were driven into dozens of leaks in the riddled bulkheads and hull; the gangway doors lying under the surface were sealed and bulkheads shored up. The jobs seemed to be endless, but the divers and salvage men made such progress that it surprised even the salvage officer.

The absence of light in the ship was a big handicap; the debris floating about in the cabins obstructed the divers; but the worst drawback was the fuel oil which sullied everything it touched and fouled the hands and faces and clothes of the salvors. Sometimes they resembled devils straight out of the inferno, yet they toiled away cheerfully in spite of the muck. They were a magnificent team and I am glad to pay them tribute.

Placing the pumps gave the salvage officer a bit of a headache. Unable to find direct entries for them in the compartments where they were wanted, he was obliged to order the use of oxyacetylene cutters to make a way for the pumps through the obstructing metal. It was a filthy job, but the salvage men did it cheerfully. The steep slope of the deck often made them struggle for a foothold; at times they were forced to work in spaces so cramped that they could hardly move; but they got through their manifold tasks as quickly as the divers accomplished theirs.

By October 7 they were approaching the climax when the pumps could test their work, as well as the calculations of the salvage officer. Until he had pumped out thousands of tons of water from the stern and started to refloat that end, he was obliged to leave the forward holds untouched to keep her anchored to the reef. Had he attempted to refloat the bow first, she might have got out of control and overturned.

At that crisis he longed for a few more pumps. A couple of twelve-inch motor pumps each throwing out about 700 tons of water an hour would have simplified things, while two or three electric submersible pumps would have been a godsend, for he could have dropped them right to the bottom of the ship and avoided the trouble of moving them once they were properly placed. As it was, the ship was over fifty feet deep, and the pumps on which he relied could not lift the water for more than twenty-six feet. This meant that after they had reduced the level of the water inside the compartments and holds to about the halfway mark, the pumps would have to be dropped to a lower level to pump out the water that remained. Manhandling pumps in those conditions was no light work.

With the eight-inch pump to take care of No. 8 hold, a six-inch motor pump in No. 7 hold, a six-inch and ten-inch motor pump in the engine room and a six-inch motor pump in the auxiliary room, the salvage officer gave the order on October 9 to make a test. The pumps soon gave proof that they were equal to the task. Next day, October 10, the pumps were started in earnest and began to pour hundreds of tons of water out of the ship. As the level of the water fell, the divers busied themselves inside and outside the ship looking for leaks and stopping them.

To allow the water to flow to the pumps, the divers inside the ship had to open the watertight doors, otherwise the water might have been trapped in some compartments, straining or bursting the bulkheads. As the water flowed to the pumps it naturally carried with it all the smashed furniture and fittings. The amount of debris was colossal. It consisted of everything portable in the liner, bedding, linen, broken furniture, paneling, all the stuff destroyed by fire and water. The divers were fighting incessantly to keep the pumps from being choked with it.

By the end of the first day the three top decks, A, B, and C, had been pumped out. The liner, as we know, was heeling badly. Therefore the weight of water on the high side of the ship was automatically reduced, while the weight of water in the lower side exerted a tendency to pull her down and overturn her. Commander Wheeler, fully alive to the danger, stopped the pumps occasionally to allow the water in these lower compartments to be drained off.

All night and all next day the pumps were kept running. The men toiled without stopping through the following night, struggling to shift pumps to a lower level as the water dropped, with the divers striving continually to keep the pumps clear. By midday on October 12, when the exhausted men had been working without rest for eighty-four hours, the stern of the liner had slowly lifted nine feet to prove that she was regaining buoyancy. That day was Sunday, and during the morning the dining room amidships had been pumped out, although the lower side of it was still under seven feet of water owing to the way she was heeling. The water which shallowed up to the center of the dining room was entirely covered with oil. The part of the deck which sloped upward out of the water was a mass of charred wood and charcoal spread in a dense layer up to six inches thick.

At two-thirty in the afternoon the room was inspected and its condition noted. The charred wood underfoot testified to the fierceness of the fire which had raged there. After a brief look round to see how things were shaping, the salvage officer withdrew to see how the work was progressing elsewhere.

At three o'clock someone noticed smoke coming out of the dining room. The salvage men rushed to see what had happened. To their surprise, the whole place was ablaze. At once the salvage ship brought her fire hoses into action, and it was three hours before the fire was put out.

Its cause remained a mystery. Was it possible that some embers of charcoal at the bottom of that dense mass had remained alive after being weeks under water? Fire cannot burn without oxygen. Whether sufficient oxygen could have been trapped in that mat of charcoal to keep a few embers at the bottom alive, and whether the density of the dried charcoal sealed off the water from the lowest layer is more than I can tell. Fire must have come into contact with the oil to cause the blaze; and as matches and cigarettes were ruled out, this suggestion may be a solution to the mystery, unless the sun's rays falling on a piece of glass acted as a burning glass and ignited the oil. Anyway, I have been amazed myself to find hot embers tucked away in a burned-out heap of garden rubbish that has been subjected to constant heavy rain for two or three days, and these embers have started to glow as soon as the wind blew on them, although I would have sworn that the rain had extinguished everything.

After that fiery interlude the men spent the next ten or twelve days shifting the pumps into various compartments and lowering them as the level of the water decreased. Though much water still remained in her, the liner was fully buoyant, and at two-thirty on the afternoon of October 27 the bow of the *Georgic* was hauled off the coral reef by the salvage ship.

The salvors were mystified to find that water was still leaking into the vessel, notwithstanding that the divers had carefully patched, plugged, and wedged all the damage they could find in the hull. Juggling with their cement, they toiled to make the hull tight. To their annoyance the water seeped through in numerous places to wash the cement away before it could set. The divers had done a first-class job. Their work throughout was beyond praise. Yet the seepage proved that there was something wrong somewhere.

It was, indeed — though the cause rather taxed credulity. To suggest that lots of hungry little fishes might have nibbled away at the liner until they had nibbled her to the bottom again appears to be the fishiest story of all time. Yet it is based on more truth than is apparent in many angling stories.

In order to make sure that all their wedges and plugs were watertight, the divers went to the trouble of forcing tallow all round them to stop any tiny orifices through which the water might filter. This tallow evidently tickled the palates of the fish in the bay, for they came in their multitudes to feast off it and suck it out of the crevices. Thus these shoals of little fish added to the worries of the men inside the ship who kept seeing their cement seeping away before it could harden.

The worst damage of all running for forty feet from the front of the bridge towards the stern was overcome by the carpenters who built a gigantic box inside the ship against the distorted hull. This box was about fifty feet long, ten feet high and four feet wide. When finished it was filled with concrete which made a mighty patch quite impervious to the sea: it gave the weakened hull all the support that it needed.

By November 18 Commander Wheeler was able to return to Alexandria to take charge of other salvage operations, leaving his assistant salvage officer, Captain W. H. Rogers, to add the finishing touches to the *Georgic*. Eleven days later, on November 29, the burned-out liner was handed over to the Cunard officials.

Because men must eat to live, a great electric oven was installed in the *Georgic* to cook for the men who would be in charge of her while she was being towed to Bombay. That oven was heated by the current supplied by the portable generator, and it provided a perfect means of insuring that the farm tractor and generator were kept in excellent order during the voyage.

A Clan liner towed her out of Suez and down the Red Sea for about seven hundred miles to Port Sudan. Then the liner was recalled to Alexandria to help to make up a fast convoy to replace one that had been severely mauled in its attempt to run supplies through to Malta. Unfortunately the Clan liner which towed the *Georgic* on the first leg of her long voyage to Bombay was sunk during that run to Malta.

The *Georgic* eventually reached Bombay and in the end steamed back to England at fifteen knots under her own power. After being refitted, she played a big part in carrying home troops after the war, and in 1951 she plied between New York and Southampton as a one-class ship ferrying visitors to and from the Festival of Britain.

CHAPTER VI

The Port of London's Ordeal

THOSE six ships sunk by magnetic mines in the Thames estuary on that November day of 1939 gave a dramatic warning of the enemy's intentions to try to block the channels leading to the Port of London so that the widespread system of docks supplying the teeming millions of the metropolis could be brought to a standstill. Convinced that to sink a ship anywhere at sea would sap Great Britain's strength, the Germans from the beginning were determined to pursue this aim night and day. None recognized more clearly than the enemy that it was even more desirable to sink ships in the channels leading to British ports, for by so doing they reaped a double dividend and robbed the country of shipping and port facilities at the same time. The approaches to the ports were thus ideal areas in which to sow mines, and a successful attempt to choke the channels of the Thames would assuredly paralyze the Port of London.

Fully alive to the menace, the Port of London Authority was determined to prevent the Germans from achieving their object. The danger was marked by the Admiralty who arranged with the port authorities to grapple with all the wrecks in the river Thames and out beyond the Nore to a line extending from Walton on the Naze and along the coast of northern Kent to the North Foreland. As salvage plant and vessels became available, the peacetime equipment of the port authorities was augmented by the Admiralty to meet the growing needs.

The burden of this salvage work fell upon Captain R.

Brooks, who, having served with the Liverpool and Glasgow Salvage Association and dealt with wrecks for the Admiralty in the First World War, had spent the intervening years steaming up and down the river from Tower Bridge to the Nore, giving a hand to ships in distress and helping to lift a wreck out of the way to keep the channels clear. Limehouse Reach and Long Reach were as familiar to him as his back garden, and he knew all the shoals and buoys and lights better than his own face, for he saw them more often. He knew, too, how much help he could expect from the tide when he was on a lifting job and how far the run of the tide would allow him to tow a cripple in safety before beaching her. It was priceless knowledge that served the nation well during those bleak years when the enemy strove by every means within his power to knock out the Port of London. As Mooring and Wreck Raising Officer of the port authorities, Captain Brooks was indefatigable in his efforts to defeat the German aim. Captain J. N. Edwards, who joined him early in 1940 to assist in his duties, succeeded him when the war was over.

The war years were crowded with adventures that often touched the peak of excitement between lulls that were heavy with unknown threats. No one knew what would happen next. Often the expected and the unexpected happened simultaneously and called for prompt measures to cope with them. The River Department which handled the traffic flowing in and out of the port was organized on a twenty-four hours' basis, with responsible officers on duty day and night throughout the war to deal with any emergency that might arise. They knew what to do and did it without hesitation.

For instance, one Saturday afternoon an officer was alone in his office, within sight of Tower Bridge, dealing with the papers on his desk, when he heard a bang. It was no uncommon sound in those tense days, with bombs falling and guns breaking the silence at all times, so he paid little attention to it and went on working. Suddenly the door opened and a lone colleague on duty in another department poked in his head. "Hear that bang?" asked the newcomer.

"Yes. What was it?"

"A ship mined — down at Bellamy's Wharf."

Bellamy's Wharf was but a stone's throw from the Tower of London, and for the Germans to drop a mine there was a tribute to their enterprise and marksmanship. The officer wasted no time in useless speculation. Picking up the telephone, he called Captain Brooks at his home down the river. "A ship has just sat on a mine down at Bellamy's Wharf," he said.

"I'll come at once," was the response of the salvage officer, who immediately jumped into his car and drove down to Greenwich, where he stepped into a speedboat and rushed upstream to find that the steamer *Grenaa* had sunk beside the wharf with a cargo of grain. Putting first things first, the salvage officer turned his attention to saving as much of the cargo as possible, and his swift action with the pumps resulted in the recovery of 1500 tons of undamaged grain. A little later on he picked the steamer up to clear the wharf for other vessels and towed her down-river where he beached her to give the shipwrights a chance of making temporary repairs. These done, he hauled her off at high tide and towed her to dry dock where she was put in order again.

To pick up that wreck he had to go west almost to the doorstep of his headquarters. To deal with the collier *Dagenham* in November 1940 he had to steam down-river beyond the Nore lightship to the East Cant Sands where the unlucky ship had hit a mine and foundered off the Isle of Sheppey. Sending the divers down to survey the damage, he set them to work patching and plugging, and when they were ready he installed his pumps to refloat her.

While pumping was going on, a German aircraft began to circle overhead. The salvage officer did not like it. The enemy seemed to be taking too much interest in them. Knowing what it portended, he did not dally. As soon as the *Dagenham* was well afloat and under control, he towed her away to the Jenkin Sands. It was well that he did so, for that night the German bombers came across and dropped flares all over the position where the wreck had been in an endeavor to locate her and give her the finishing touch. But she was gone — another ship saved to serve the Allied cause, thanks to the salvage officer.

It was a mile or two away on the West Cant Sands that the motor vessel *Attendant* was mined and sent to the bottom. She was an Admiralty oiler of just over a thousand tons, and the naval authorities at nearby Sheerness were dubious about her recovery. They thought she had received her deathblow. The salvage officer thought otherwise. He listened to the reports of the divers and concluded that she could be saved.

The mouth of the Medway and the waters round Sheerness had a particular attraction for the enemy. They knew that if they sowed their mines in the neighborhood there was always the chance of an important kill near the naval dockyard. This made things no easier for the salvage officer and added more than a spice of danger for the divers. From time to time a mine exploded in the vicinity, setting up a shock wave that would have been fatal to any diver in the danger zone. Despite the risk, diver E. Bland held resolutely to his task and carried on with the underwater work until it was completed. After the salvage officer could get his pumps into position, he refloated the *Attendant* and towed her upriver to Millwall dry dock where she was repaired and put into commission again. The salvage officer's flair for the work saved the ship and the diver's courage won him the British Empire Medal for diving under such risky conditions.

When Goering in his arrogance let loose his bombers to carry out his plan of effacing the docks of London, he sent over his great air fleets in broad daylight to spread destruction far and wide. The targets were so vast and so plainly grouped along the river, which acted as a pointer to them, that the enemy could not fail to see them and find the mark with some of his bombs.

Fortunately for London and the whole of civilization, Goering underestimated the hitting power of the British fighter pilots who wrought such havoc among the German bombers that he was forced to call off the daylight attacks and switch to night bombing. A fighter pilot of those days described to me how in one of the first big daylight attacks over the Thames a pilot of his squadron performed the extraordinary feat of shooting down three bombers in a single burst of fire. The bombers started fires which were not easily subdued and the firemen were on duty till they dropped with fatigue.

One blazing oil tank became a pillar of flame to guide the bombers in at night. The enemy took full advantage of such guides to plaster the docks with hundreds of high explosive bombs and thousands of incendiary bombs, and there were never-to-be-forgotten nights when the whole of Thames-side appeared to be a blazing inferno. Barges were sunk, wharves and docks had great gaps blown in them, and warehouses packed with priceless commodities belched smoke and flame to the heavens and continued to smolder for weeks.

London in those days was indeed a city of dreadful nights, but the salvage service under Captain Brooks operated efficiently throughout. During the magnetic-mine attack in the third week of November 1939 shipping suffered some delay until a safe passage was insured, yet not for a single day, even when the air attacks were at their zenith, did the Port of London cease to operate. In their prudence the P.L.A. wisely deflected a good deal of shipping to other ports that were not subject to such risks. Traffic at times was curtailed to a third of its normal capacity, but throughout the war the ships steamed in and out of the Thames, and never once did the Germans entirely succeed in blocking the port, although sometimes it was a close thing.

Barges were set ablaze and sunk all over the place, alongside the wharves and out in the river. When the sinkings were reported, the salvage officers went off with their lifting lighters and pumps to raise the ships, selecting those that were obstructing the wharves before dealing with those in other parts of the river that were not interfering with unloading facilities.

The salvage vessel *Yantlet* could lift 120 tons over the bows if necessary; but to deal with the dead weight of a big ship the salvage crew generally used two big pontoons, or camels, which between them could lift a weight of 2400 tons, after the divers had passed the lifting wires under the wreck and clamped them to the pontoons. These were invaluable when it came to lifting a wreck out of the fairway and putting her on the beach for further attention.

For instance, in 1941 a German mine planted most skillfully from the air just off Becton Jetty in Gallions Reach sent the collier *Halo* to the bottom. As she sank she swung across the channel and caused considerable obstruction. The salvage officer was soon on the scene shifting the cargo into lighters. As soon as he had lightened her sufficiently, the divers slipped the wires underneath her and she was lifted and beached at Woolwich. With the channel cleared, the salvage officer was able to leave her in the hands of the shipwrights who patched her up before she was towed to dry dock for permanent repairs.

There was excitement and to spare when the *Colonel Crompton* was set on fire by the enemy in the Thames estuary. The salvage ships, coming to her aid, were greeted with exploding ammunition. It did not stop them. Heedless of the risk, two of the men jumped aboard to fight the fire, and their efforts, which won decorations, enabled the vessel to be brought safely to the Royal Albert Dock.

Another German mine hit the tanker *Josefina Thorden* off Harwich and did such damage that it broke her in half. The stern sank, leaving the bow adrift. In due course the Ad-

miralty tugs took charge of the bow and began to tow it to
Shell Haven, a short distance above Hole Haven in Canvey
Island, where many a pretty piece of smuggling took place in
olden days.

During the tow the weather turned nasty. The tugs did
their best to keep going, but in the rising gale the bow of the
tanker became unmanageable and was driven hard ashore on
the East Spile Sands. Though only half a ship, she was nevertheless worth a fortune, for she was full of 4900 tons of solid
lubricating oil base that was due to be treated in the Shell
Refinery at Shell Haven. This solidified lubricant was of the
utmost importance to the war effort, and Captain Brooks hurried to the scene in the salvage ship *King Lear* to see what was
to be done.

To haul her off in her heavily laden state was a difficult
operation. There was, however, another way of dealing with
the wreck. To the logical salvage officer it was obvious that a
solid lubricant could be melted with heat, and if melted it
would become liquid, and if liquefied it could be pumped out
without difficulty. Calling up a naval tanker, the salvage officer
introduced a steam pipe into the tanks of the wreck, and as
the steam melted the lubricant the pumps sucked it into the
oiler alongside. As soon as he had pumped out enough to serve
his purpose, he hauled the bow off the sands and towed her to
Shell Haven where the rest of the cargo was unloaded. The
efficiency of the salvage men may be judged when it is known
that during these difficult operations no more than thirty-one
tons of the cargo was lost, while the cargo saved was valued
at £250,000.

At the best of time dredgers are unwieldy things to handle
and if they happen to sink they may cause endless trouble,
even in tidal waters where the lift of the tide may be relied
upon to help the salvage officer in his task. A dredger which
the authority used for dredging ballast from the channels
happened to be in Greenland Dock when a bombing attack

developed and a bomb crashed right through her and took her to the bottom.

As soon as the salvage officer heard of the casualty he knew that there was no tide in the dock to assist him. But he had his lifting craft and had no doubt that they would soon do the trick for him as they had done many times before. When, at length, he got his lifting wires in place and pumped out his lifting craft, he discovered that although by all the rules she ought to have come up without much trouble, she simply refused to budge.

The mud had got her firmly in its grip. The suction exerted such a powerful hold on her that he could not shift her. It was as though she were cemented to the bottom.

"Why not dig a hole in the mud to break the suction?" someone suggested. It seemed a simple remedy.

Accordingly, a hole was scooped in the mud under her stern and more mud was grabbed out alongside the hull.

It worked miraculously. The dredge came up like a bird and was carried off for permanent repairs. Before the end of the year she was back again on her old job.

While the salvage officers were grappling with war casualties, the usual marine casualties kept cropping up from time to time to add to their work. For instance the *Moscha D. Kydoniefs*, a steamer of 3784 tons, passed up the Thames on Sunday, May 9, 1943, with a cargo of 6000 tons of grain in her holds and eight tanks and two aircraft stowed on her decks. Steaming quietly along Erith Reach, where Erith marshes sliding away to starboard were soon succeeded by Plumstead marshes, she turned into Barking Reach. She was almost at her journey's end when, just off Woolwich Arsenal and opposite the entrance to George V Dock, she came into collision with another vessel. There was the rending and grinding of metal on metal as a huge hole forty-eight feet long by twenty-five feet deep opened up in her hull and she settled down.

Captain Brooks was soon on the spot, and early next morning the salvage men started on the task of lightening the wreck. Bringing up their floating derricks, they fixed slings under the tanks and lifted them out one by one. Then they picked up the two aircraft and placed them in safety. With these valuable weapons salved, they began to lift out the spare parts of trucks until they had recovered 272 tons, after which they dropped their pumps into the holds and started to discharge the undamaged grain into barges alongside the wreck.

As soon as the salvage officer had reduced her weight to manageable proportions, he pinned down his lifting craft at the ebb of the tide, and as she came up on the rising tide he hauled her ashore at Woolwich and beached her on top of the tide so that she could no longer interfere with the river traffic.

During the intervals of dealing with these urgent cases there were five wrecks which had been cluttering up parts of the Thames estuary and restricting the channel enough to cause disquiet to the Commander in Chief, Nore. The wrecks were not particularly large: they ranged from a tug of 196 tons to a steamer of just over a thousand tons. They were nevertheless in the way and a threat to other ships that might wander slightly off course in a fog, so Captain Brooks was charged with the duty of removing them. As ships their day was done; so, when opportunity served, the salvage crews lifted great chunks of them and planted them on the beach off Southend to feed Britain's voracious scrap furnaces.

Another little job which engaged the salvage men at the Nore in the summer of 1943 was the steamer *Bolbec*, which complicated matters by overturning as she sank. They got their wires under her and carried her, still overturned, to Southend where they beached her before pulling her upright.

These were but a few of the cases which the salvage officers and crews were called upon to tackle in those desperate days. Sometimes things slipped and men were hurt, but no one was seriously injured and not a single life was lost despite the danger of the work. From the beginning to the end of the war the salvage department of the Port of London Authority raised thirty-six ships of 83,811 tons, while they helped forty-six other ships that were in difficulties. In between these major cases were the minor cases that were always cropping up in the docks and the river, a tug sunk here, a barge there, and a launch elsewhere. Altogether the small craft raised numbered 340, so in defeating the German attempt to knock out the Port of London the salvage officers and men of the Port of London Authority did much to bring the enemy to ultimate defeat.

CHAPTER VII

The Suez Canal Crisis

RANKING as one of the world's greatest engineering feats, the digging of the Suez Canal by Ferdinand de Lesseps through the desert from the Red Sea to Port Said was a stroke of genius designed to save the long passage round the Cape of Good Hope to India by making a short cut east through the Mediterranean Sea. As for Disraeli's purchase of 176,692 Suez Canal shares from the Khedive of Egypt in 1875, it combined statesmanship with a business acumen of the highest order. The loss and dislocation imposed by a holdup in the canal in peacetime was brought home to Great Britain and other countries when the Egyptians illegally prevented the passage of British oil tankers to the Haifa Refinery in 1950.

Few people, least of all De Lesseps, could have imagined that this vital artery from West to East would ever become a vital artery from the West to Egypt. While Great Britain held Gibraltar, the gateway to the Mediterranean was safe. But the immobilization of the French navy after the fall of France allowed Italy to dominate the Mediterranean with her navy and air force, and consequently the only safe way to send troops and munitions to Egypt was round by the Cape and northward through the Suez Canal. To maintain a free flow of ships through the canal was of paramount importance to Britain's war effort, while the blocking of the canal for any length of time would have threatened a disaster of the first magnitude.

With great daring, General Wavell on December 10, 1940, with his small force of 35,000 men, fell upon Graziani's armies which had penetrated into Egypt and by December 16, 1940, had driven them back with a loss of 40,000 men as well as immense supplies collected for the proposed march to Cairo. That was the first triumph of the forty-seven Matilda tanks which were secretly rushed to Egypt to confound the enemy. Following up this victory, Wavell harried the enemy until Graziani was driven back to Benghazi. On February 4, 1941, General O'Connor ordered the tanks of the Seventh Armored Division to find a way across an unknown and difficult stretch of desert to make their remarkable inland march which cut the line of the Italian retreat along the coast road and led to the resounding victory of Beda Fomm, where British tanks forced the complete surrender of the Italian armies.

On the very morning that the British tank force started on its victorious dash across the desert, the steamship *Ranee* cast off in ballast at Port Said just before midday to make her way with a convoy through the Suez Canal to Suez. Reaching the halfway mark at Ismailia on the shore of Lake Timsah, she dropped anchor for the night with the rest of the ships and at 8:30 next morning got under way again, the thirteenth ship in the convoy. She had been steaming little more than half an hour when she shuddered under the shock of a big explosion and sank on the sandy bottom on the western side of the canal with a vast hole near her stern.

One of the magnetic mines dropped by raiders during the night had found its mark. They were not the first raiders to attack the canal, though they were the first to create trouble. The defenses of this vital link were anything but strong. At intervals of about a quarter of a mile the Egyptians had insisted on making sandbag shelters along the banks of the canal in which four or five men were posted to defend the waterway. The most that can be said was that it was a token defense, for many of the men were armed with staves and broomsticks, although here and there was a man with a rifle. One Egyptian who fired his rifle in a futile attempt to hit a raiding aircraft was promoted to the rank of sergeant on the spot. As for anti-aircraft guns along the banks of the canal, there was at the time a general shortage.

The authorities, alive to the danger, promptly moored the wreck of the *Ranee* to the bank to prevent her from moving farther into the fairway. At any time a wreck in the canal was a grave danger to shipping, but at that particular time it threatened to block the main lifeline which carried all the supplies to the British armies in Egypt.

A few hours later, when the convoy was steaming about thirty miles farther on, a Greek steamer, the *Agios Georgius,* struck another mine and sank about twelve miles from Suez. She was in a far worse plight than the *Ranee,* for it transpired that her back was broken in two places. As the bottom of the canal thereabouts was rock, the use of a dredge could not remedy matters.

The normal procedure when two ships wished to pass each other was for one to tie up to the bank and allow the other to go by. The navigable channel in the center of the canal provided ample room for one ship, but it was not wide enough for two. The bottom of the canal resembled a saucer in which the dredges were continually at work replacing on the banks the sand washed down into the main channel.

On the day the *Ranee* and *Agios Georgius* sank, the resounding victory of Beda Fomm struck a cheering note throughout Egypt and Great Britain. Heartened by his crushing victories, Wavell pushed his units forward until they reached the limit of their advance at El Agheila. At this juncture, when the whole of North Africa appeared to be falling into Wavell's hands, the German threat to Greece grew so serious that he and his advisers were forced to decide whether the British Government should implement its earlier promise to send a force of Imperial troops with British armor to the aid of Greece, or whether that gallant people who had given Mussolini's armies such a trouncing should be left to their fate. To the honor of Great Britain the decision was made to stand by Greece with all available forces, notwithstanding that it weakened the formations in the desert and made the forward positions up to El Agheila with their long supply line very vulnerable.

A bare week after the British armor had crushed the Italian tanks and troops at Beda Fomm, Rommel appeared in North Africa to try to avenge Graziani's defeat. Unobtrusively, he gathered his force of some three hundred tanks and spent the remaining days of February brooding over his plans. While he prepared to fall on El Agheila at the end of March, the German forces gathering in Bulgaria made ready to strike at Greece early in April.

The Suez Canal was vital. Through it flowed the troops and tanks and guns and shells and motor transport and vast quantities of supplies to keep the armies in being. Sir Winston Churchill had firsthand knowledge of its importance. "The vulnerability of the Suez Canal to magnetic and acoustic mines gave cause for much anxiety just when these big movements of troops and convoys was starting," he wrote in volume three * of "The Second World War."

At that critical moment when ships were urgently required to move tanks and troops to the help of Greece, the enemy succeeded in his attempts to block the Suez Canal by dropping mines from aircraft. It was a shrewd blow, perfectly timed and cleverly delivered. The lifeline of the armies in the Middle East was completely cut. The ships fitted to carry motor transport and tanks were gathered at the northern end of the canal at Port Said, while the troopships were held up at the southern end at Suez. It was a menacing situation. All the ships of the Royal Navy were virtually trapped in the Mediterranean. There was no line of escape for them through the Suez Canal if they were suddenly assailed by overwhelming air

* *The Grand Alliance.*

power and found it necessary to get away for permanent repairs.

On March 5, the very day that the first troops were being embarked at the Mediterranean end to succor Greece, Commander G. J. Wheeler arrived at Suez on his way to take up the appointment of Fleet Salvage Officer to the Mediterranean Fleet at Alexandria. He was given no time to continue his journey. Seized upon as soon as he arrived by the naval officer in charge, he was promptly sent along by car to deal with the *Ranee*. It was imperative that the wreck should be moved out of the way, for the Suez Canal was the only safe channel through which Wavell's armies could be sustained. The single railway line from Suez to Cairo was quite inadequate to handle this gigantic traffic. Port Tewfik at Suez lacked the facilities to deal with the mass of shipping. As for the narrow road leading from Suez across the desert to Ismailia, its surface was made up by spreading the oily residues from the local oil refinery over the desert sand, so its limitations can be imagined.

Nor were the *Ranee* and *Agios Georgius* the only obstructions in the canal, for dotted along its course were a number of smaller craft which had fallen victims. The Germans were fully alive to the fact that the Suez Canal was the main artery carrying the lifeblood of the British armies in the Middle East, and they were determined to block it permanently if they could. They also knew, what the British intelligence officers were doing their best to learn, the exact day and hour when Rommel would pounce on El Agheila and the German armies would be let loose against Greece, so they could drop their mines in the canal at the moment when they would cause the utmost dislocation. The news of their success was as unwelcome in London as it was at headquarters in the Middle East.

Arriving at the wreck of the *Ranee*, Commander Wheeler found the bow jutting up and twisted from the mainmast like a pugilist's nose that had failed to straighten out after a terrific side punch. Water lapped about the poop deck, which meant about forty feet of water over the side. The after deck was ten feet below the surface. An examination revealed that the engine room was flooded, there was a nasty leak in one of the bulkheads, and part of the deck had been blown up by the explosion. Much of the hull where the mine struck was blown away, but the ship lay in such a position that the diver was defeated in all attempts to discover the extent of the damage underneath her.

There the *Ranee* lay just as she had sunk a month earlier. No attempt had been made to deal with her. The canal authorities, restrained by the uncertainties of the legal position, were afraid that if an attempt were made to raise her, the top hamper might make her topple over and form an impassable barrier to shipping. This was the present danger — that she might overturn and complicate a position that was already grave.

To the experienced eyes of the salvage officer it was obvious that before any real effort could be made to shift the wreck it would be necessary to cut away the funnel, remove the bridge, and take out the mainmast. With these deck masses out of the way, the final step would be to cut the ship in half where the mines struck.

Going over the wreck with the canal engineer the next day, Commander Wheeler said: "If you cut her there" — pointing to the spot where the ship was almost broken — "the forepart can be towed to Lake Timsah and the machinery could be used for a new ship."

The overriding necessity was to get the ships moving again through the canal to reduce the mass of shipping that had collected at each end. This overshadowed everything else. It was fortunate that the *Ranee* had gone down at a spot where there was a sandy bottom, for it enabled the dredges to widen the canal at this point to allow the ships to creep past the wreck. Meanwhile some divers with their gear were rushed down by road from Port Said and when they arrived the salvage officer set them to work cutting away the top hamper and taking such emergency precautions as were essential. After three hectic days a passage was opened up to allow the convoys to bypass the wreck, and the salvage officer had the satisfaction of seeing seventy-one ships steam across the desert to Port Said to build up Wavell's strength, while forty-two vessels made the journey south to Suez. It was a brilliant accomplishment.

The *Ranee*, however, still had to be reckoned with. While some divers ate their way through the steel plates of the double bottom, others concentrated on sealing all the fractures and stopping innumerable leaks made by the explosion. As the work progressed, the watertight door of the tunnel was repaired and the fractured valves made tight.

Sweating away at a couple of twelve-inch motor pumps, the salvors jockeyed them into position in the engine room to make a test. The pumps were not long in demonstrating that they could deal with the leakage and bring the forward part of the ship, which was three hundred feet long, up on an even keel.

Notwithstanding that the divers forged ahead as fast as they could, the cutting of the bottom was a lengthy job, so was the removal of the funnel and masts and other top gear. There was enough work for a large gang of salvage workers; but the skilled men were not available and preparations for raising the forepart were slowed down considerably by the lack of experienced labor.

To give them their due, those on the job worked without respite. Nineteen days after Commander Wheeler first surveyed the wreck on March 5, the fore end was quite severed from the stern, the leaks were patched and plugged, bulkheads were shored, and the bow was made ready for pumping out. The essentials lacking were some six-inch pumps to assist the big motor pumps to overcome the water in the machinery space. By the end of the day, however, these pumps arrived and were at once placed in position.

Checking up early on March 25 to ensure that everything was in order, the salvage officer gave the signal at 8:30 in the morning to start the twelve-inch pumps. Before long the bow of the ship became alive and started to float on an even keel as the salvage officer had planned.

Of a sudden, disaster threatened. While the salvage men were struggling to get her under control, a large convoy of seventeen ships came into sight from the south, on their way to Port Said. They came without warning. Steaming at five or six knots, they created a wash that looked like the undoing, in minutes, of all the toil of the past weeks. At this crisis the refloated section was absolutely unmanageable. She became so lively that she was a great threat to the salvage craft alongside. The salvage men jumped to save her. By prodigious efforts they managed to control her and moor her in an upright position close to the canal bank.

As the ships of the convoy passed about twenty feet away from the *Ranee*, some of the captains gazed from their bridges in astonishment at the Fleet Salvage Officer out there amid the desert sands.

"Hallo!" they shouted, waving their hands. "What are you doing here?"

No wonder they were amazed. The last time they had seen him he was salving their own ships on the southern coast of England. There were in that convoy no fewer than five ships that he had brought back into service after they were wrecked. Some were loaded with coal, others with oil, and the decks of most were crammed with tanks and guns, while the holds were jammed to capacity with stores and ammunition for the British armies. They reached their destination safely to reinforce the waning strength of Wavell; but who can say what might have happened if they had been held up at Port Suez because the Suez Canal was blocked?

Despite the warm and friendly greetings from the captains of the convoy, the salvage officer watched them depart with relief. Their arrival without notification had jeopardized the whole salvage operation.

If the salvage officer imagined that his troubles were over, he was very much mistaken. The six-inch pumps were of ancient vintage. They had been sent from Malta to the Canal Zone during the 1914–1918 war and had never been unpacked until the salvage officer sent his demand. By dismantling one and using its parts as spares, three were induced to function; but the strain of working all night was too much for them. The failure of one pump naturally threw more work on the others. The inflow of water began to overtake the pumping capacity. The men nursed the other pumps as best they could, but they could not prevent a second pump from failing. Then the third pump petered out, and as the water flooded in, it drowned the motor pumps and made them useless.

The salvors took no more chances. The forepart of the *Ranee* lay close to the canal bank among the salvage barges, from one of which steam was obtained to do essential work. Entering the engine room, the divers found more valves that needed attention. They cut off the ventilators and lifted out the engine-room skylight to allow the pumps to be placed where they were wanted. They did many more repairs and adjustments of a technical nature.

Determined not to be cheated by pumps a second time, the salvage officer secured two more twelve-inch pumps to bring the combined pumping capacity up to 3500 tons an hour. It was enough. By April 3 some of the pumps were started in the engine room. As the water was reduced, two of the big pumps were lowered into place and in eight hours they poured out so much water that they brought the engine room up by twelve feet. That night, after the ship was moored, it was only necessary to run a small pump now and again to keep the water down.

Next morning, another convoy of eight ships passed south on the way to Suez. This time, however, the forepart was under control and they could do no harm. By three o'clock in the afternoon the tugs moved off with this valuable half of the *Ranee* and two hours later the bow of the wreck was anchored safely in Lake Timsah.

All the salvage skill in the world was of no avail so far as the *Agios Georgius* was concerned. She was much too badly shattered to be lifted, so in due course she was cut up and removed piecemeal.

The sinking of the *Ranee* and the *Agios Georgius* in the Suez Canal on February 5, 1941, was not trumpeted to the world. The British people, knowing nothing, were spared the anxieties aroused in the minds of their leaders. But if these ships had broken their backs right across the canal they might have changed the course of history by cutting off for a crucial period the flow of troops and guns and tanks and ammunition to replace the heavy British losses which Rommel inflicted during his amazing drive from El Agheila to the Egyptian frontier in those ten disastrous days from March 31 to April 9, 1941. If ever a man arrived in the nick of time it was the Fleet Salvage Officer.

Later he was obliged to accompany the bombed *Warspite* through the canal to see that she came to no harm in making the passage. Normally there was little clearance between the keels of such big ships and the canal bottom. To bring her through on an even keel in her damaged state would have entailed the risk of her bilge keel fouling the sloping bottom in passing the remains of wrecks that were being removed. This danger was cleverly overcome by flooding her starboard tanks and emptying those on the other side. This gave her a pronounced list toward the center of the canal and tilted her up on the port side to give clearance between her curving hull and the curving bottom of the canal. She looked rather drunk and lopsided, but she passed through without mishap.

CHAPTER VIII

At Bay in Crete

WAVELL's chance to stem the tide of the German invasion of Greece with worn British tanks and New Zealand and Australian troops grew dim as events developed. The men were fighting fit, but the majority of tanks were light and some were still clogged with leaves and pine cones from the training grounds of England. When the onslaught came on April 6, 1941, the Royal Air Force could put into the air only about 80 aircraft of which no more than a dozen were up-to-date Hurricane fighters, while the Italians could muster over 300 aircraft to add to the Luftwaffe's 800 bombers and fighters. Against this overwhelming air superiority the pilots of the Royal Air Force took heavy toll, but they were swamped by numbers. The odds of 1100 to 80 were too great. Fighting like demons in the air, strafed on the ground by the Stukas, the remnants of the British air squadrons saved what they could as they withdrew.

Swept back in those April days to southern Greece, leaving a trail of worn-out tanks by the roadside, the Imperial troops lay low all day to escape discovery by German aircraft until they could be taken off at night by the navy. Many put to sea in small boats and launches to make their own way among the islands to Crete, which the Germans even then were planning to conquer by the first airborne invasion in history.

The surviving British aircraft were too few to oppose the German airmen. They were out of range of the aircraft bases in Egypt. The Luftwaffe flew practically unchallenged in the air. Risky as it was for the troops on the ground, it was sheer suicide for ships to be caught by the Heinkels and Stukas at sea. To meet the air threat the naval and other vessels were obliged to hold off by day and steal into the Greek beaches in the velvet blackness of the night to take off thousands of men who watched keenly in absolute silence for those secret signals that meant safety.

The ships converged on Suda Bay on the northern coast of Crete, warships, destroyers, submarines and merchant ships steamed to their succor. Ships loading cargo at Smyrna and other ports were requisitioned and ordered to Crete. Little craft such as caïques and motor launches owned by the fishermen along the Greek coast were bought or chartered by bands of men who struggled over the mountains and sought to escape by sea. In three tense nights the navy took off 36,000 men, and over 50,000 were rescued in all, some being carried to Crete and others direct to Egypt.

Though Greece was lost, there were hopes that Crete could be held. The British forces on the island were small. The troops snatched from Greece were without equipment. A few light tanks and half a dozen Matildas were the sole armor in Crete, while air cover depended on a mixed bag of no more than thirty aircraft.

The Royal Navy still controlled the sea, and one dark night it surprised and destroyed to the last man the seaborne German forces who hoped to surprise the island. Undeterred by this slaughter, the German High Command one lovely day in May let loose their parachute troops who fell from the heavens in a billowing cloud and, despite dire losses, managed by nightfall to capture Maleme aerodrome. That was the beginning of the conquest of Crete, though much bitter fighting followed.

With this brief outline, we may revert to the night of April 5, a few hours before the German forces poured over the Greek frontier, when the Italians launched an attack by explosive motorboats on the British cruisers in Suda Bay. Making their way through the outer defenses and speeding

under the guns of Fort Suda between the island of Suda and
the shore, the attackers traversed the length of the bay. Slipping quietly between the buoy and the beach, they got behind
the inner defenses where the cruiser *York*, waiting to be re-
fueled, was lying beside a tanker. One Italian boat succeeded in its mission of ramming the cruiser while another
sped full tilt at the tanker, with the result that cruiser and
tanker were both sunk. Another British cruiser had a lucky
escape.

Immediately the loss of the *York* was reported to Admiral
Cunningham in Alexandria, he made urgent demands to see
how long it would take to raise her. A naval constructor, who
flew up to investigate, reported that with modern salvage ap-
pliances it would take five months.

The Admiral sent for the Fleet Salvage Officer to discuss the
matter. "You might survey her," he said.

"But why go if it will take five months, sir?" queried the
salvage officer, who was fully occupied.

"I'd like you to have a look at her," replied Admiral Cunningham.

Accordingly at seven o'clock on the evening of April 7 a
Sunderland flying boat circled and landed safely in Suda Bay
with Commander Wheeler, who had been flown direct from
Alexandria to report on the cruiser's damage. The *York* was
sitting on the bottom, while her crew were in camp ashore,
carrying on as though they were still on board. The flags of
the officers were flying, boats and barges were going to and
fro, watches were being kept, prayers were held and all the
disciplinary routine of the ship was being carried out as usual.
The enemy to the north were rolling over Greece, but here
for the moment was peace.

Next morning Commander Wheeler went over the *York* to
examine her wounds. They were grievous enough, but he had
towed many a ship to port with worse. Diving conditions at
any rate were favorable, because the cruiser sat on a sandy

bottom at the western end of the bay, so there was no need for the divers to flounder about in mud and darkness. This was to the good. Her quarter-deck was about four feet above the surface and she had both boiler rooms and one engine room flooded. Noting the way in which her sides had been buckled by a stick of bombs that straddled her after she had grounded, Commander Wheeler watched the divers moving slowly about her hull as he awaited their report. As soon as they came up he learned the worst. She had a huge hole in her port side about twenty-five feet long and twelve feet high. The bilge keel had been split and driven down by the force of the explosion, and below the bilge keel the bottom was rent open, with the edges of the plates twisted in a fantastic manner, some being torn outwards and others thrust inwards.

Conning his list of damages, the salvage officer worked out how much timber would be required to cover the holes, the balks for shoring bulkheads, pumps to control the water, underwater cutters for shearing away the twisted plates to enable the ship to be patched, the plugs, pads, air compressors, and all the gear necessary to refloat her and bring her to port. He signaled his requirements to Alexandria.

The loss of the *York* was of grave concern to Admiral Sir Andrew Cunningham. To be deprived of her fire-power and speed when the cruiser strength of the navy in the Middle East was so sadly reduced added greatly to his problems. He was keen to know the earliest moment when the cruiser could be brought to Alexandria.

"It will take four weeks to refloat the ship after the gear has arrived — providing no further damage is suffered," was the gist of the salvage officer's report. In his lifetime he had performed many outstanding salvage feats that were records in their day. He had brought to port many wrecks that appeared to be doomed. And he had seen gales smash up the work of weeks and destroy the chance of saving a ship that was ready to be pumped out and towed home. In his wisdom he added the warning about further damage. In marine salvage, you never can tell.

The difference between five months and a month was so great that it aroused considerable skepticism at headquarters. "Raise her in a month, will he?" said the admiral to his staff. "We'll give him the chance to make good his word. We'll show him!"

They did. They acted in the way that has won the Royal Navy the respect of many nations. Orders were given and promptly carried out.

Imagine the amazement of the Fleet Salvage Officer when he saw the battleships *Warspite* and *Valiant* with an aircraft carrier and destroyers come steaming into Suda Bay. He was still more amazed when he found that the sacred decks of the *Warspite* were so cluttered up with air compressors, balks of timber and other salvage gear for raising the *York* that she resembled a builder's yard.

In two frantic hours the gear was dumped in a lighter while the Commander in Chief, who had come to see things for himself, went over the *York* and discussed the prospects with Commander Wheeler. Then the battleships pulled out and steamed southwards as quickly as they had come.

The day that Commander Wheeler flew from Alexandria, the salvage ship *Protector* was in Suez at the other end of the canal. An urgent message sent her steaming northward through the desert and lakes to Port Said. Putting to sea, she steamed westwards to Alexandria where she shipped a few more odds and ends of salvage gear before setting course for Crete.

While she was on her way, Commander Wheeler pushed forward with his preparations, and by April 14, when she arrived, he was ready to go ahead at full speed.

Next morning the divers began to burn through the bilge keel with their underwater cutters, for it was so distorted that no wooden patch could be made to fit closely over it without trimming away the ragged edges. They put in a full day's work with good results.

But the following day their troubles began. The weather was bad and the wind blew in such fierce gusts that the whole morning was wasted standing by. The squalls hit a Dutch steamer anchored near the *York* and made her drag her moorings. Drifting helplessly, she was in such imminent danger of crashing into the cruiser that the salvage ship had to take charge of her to prevent further damage to the *York*. While the *Protector* was grappling with the Dutch vessel to insure her safety, H.M.S. *Chakla* was caught by a gust which drove her hard ashore, whereupon the *Protector* had to link up and haul her off into deep water. That morning was full of excitement, but all work on the *York* was stopped.

No sooner had the wind died down than the Luftwaffe came along to hinder operations. It was too dangerous for divers to remain under water when enemy bombers were about, for a bomb dropped some distance away might easily have caused a fatal concussion. The rule was that at the first sound of an air-raid warning the divers had to be drawn up. Three raids during the rest of the day robbed the divers of three precious hours of work. They made up for lost time in the intervals by doggedly cutting away a mass of the bilge keel weighing three tons to smooth the way for the patch that was to follow.

Diving soon after daylight next morning, they started to burn off still more distorted edges of the plates to make a flat surface for the planks to bed down on. The German pilots, seeing the salvage ship and diving boats round the cruiser, quickly sensed what was going on. They were determined to stop it if they could. Flying over, they dropped their loads of bombs, but their marksmanship that day was none too good and the nearest they got to the *York* was 500 feet.

Early the following morning the salvage men, working on

the deck of the cruiser, began to build a section of the wooden patch some nine feet long, while the divers below manipulated the first plank into place and bolted it home through the hull. By the end of the day they had managed to fit another plank and make it ready to receive the section of the patch which was lying on deck waiting to be lowered over the side for the divers to maneuver and bolt into position. When work ceased, it seemed fairly certain that the first section of the patch would be fixed next day. Yet in marine salvage nothing is certain. The patch, weighted at the lower edge to keep it upright, was swung outboard on the derrick and gently lowered to the divers, who guided it into place over the part of the hole it was made to fit. With deft fingers they secured it by two or three bolts to hold it in position. Before they could fit the full quota of bolts an air-raid warning compelled them to knock off.

The guns started up as German aircraft flew over the shipping and hurled down their bombs. One bomber got a direct hit on the Greek steamer *Ithaki*, which was soon blazing fiercely. The valves of another Greek steamer were shattered by a near miss, and the sea began to pour into the engine room. To save her, the divers from the *York*, were obliged to devote their skill to plugging the holes, otherwise she would have sunk. This first-aid work coupled with two more bombing raids stopped them from fixing the patch on the *York* that day. During the raid-free intervals, however, the shipwrights on the *York* succeeded in making another section of the patch ready for the divers to tackle.

Making the most of their opportunity next morning, the divers bolted the first patch home. Having brought their under-water cutters into play to burn away a few more ragged edges, they signaled up for the next patch. Guiding it deftly into place, they fitted it in. While they were engaged on this task, the shipwrights on deck were completing the next section.

The German bombers, bent on their deadly work, gave them no rest. From time to time the guns opened up as the bombers made their run in, forcing the divers to come up to shelter in the cruiser. About ten o'clock in the morning another bomb caught the burned-out steamer and took her to the bottom. At midday a further raid brought trouble to a third steamer, for a bomb went right through her side and landed in her hold. But luck was with her, and it failed to explode. However, she flooded at such a rate that she had to be run ashore to save her.

Yet in spite of all these risks and delays the salvage officer was pleased with the progress made on the *York*. Summing up the work, he reckoned to finish the patching in three days and have the cruiser ready for pumping out by April 24. He was proud of the men who worked for him. They were craftsmen who took pride in their work and their one desire was to finish the job in the shortest time and see their ship towed into dock. Dangers beset them from air and sea. They never quailed. They were a well-trained team, much too sensible to do fool-hardy things. Yet when occasion demanded they could rise to heights of great courage to bring their ship safely home.

"Three days and she will be fit for pumping," thought Commander Wheeler as he turned in to sleep that night.

By half-past six on the morning of April 22 they were on the job again. A diver, fiitting one or two bolts to the last section of the patch, rose to the surface when he had finished. Another section of the patch was lying on the deck, ready to be lowered over the hole.

Just after nine o'clock the diver from the salvage ship *Protector* stood on the ladder of the diving boat while his attendant screwed up the glass of his helmet. The air was blown through to see that the air pipe and valves were clear, as is the usual routine, then he received the recognized tap on the helmet to tell him all was well, and he took the shot rope in his hands and slid to the bottom. On the deck of the other diving boat a naval diver was dressed ready to go down when the air-raid warning sounded.

The attendant immediately gave the regulation four pulls on the breast rope of the *Protector*'s diver to tell him to come up. The diver wasted no time in obeying the signal. His attendant quickly unscrewed his helmet and began to remove his diving suit. The other attendant acted just as promptly to strip the suit from the naval diver.

Barely a minute after the first diver was drawn up, a bomber dropped a bomb about fifty feet away. Close in the wake of the first bomber another dropped a stick of bombs which straddled the *York*. One bomb struck the sea no more than five feet from the diving boats. It simply blew them out of the water and turned them bottom up.

Commander Wheeler, who was only ten feet distant up on the deck of the *York*, had a remarkable escape. Leading his men to the rescue, he helped to haul the diver out of the water. Despite their devoted efforts to revive him, the diver was already dead. The other diver had vanished. Thinking he was under the upturned boat, they righted her, but could find no trace of him. Most of the diving crew were injured in some way or another, one attendant having a broken leg and the other being wounded in the head.

A sad tragedy to the families that were left behind, it was something of a disaster to the salvage crew of the *Protector*. The divers were the key men. They had been wiped out in a moment. Their tragic death imperiled the whole salvage operation.

The ships moored round the cruiser did not escape. The *Protector* herself suffered considerable damage; an oil tanker lying astern of the *York* got a direct hit which sank her, while an army landing craft nearby was badly shaken up.

At dusk that evening, after recurring air raids, a plucky diver volunteered to go down to see what had happened to the cruiser. Three times the air-raid warnings sounded and three times he had to be brought to the surface. It says much for his courage that he persisted in his attempts so soon after his colleagues had been killed. During his survey of the ship he had the nerve-racking experience of meeting with the dead diver whose body he recovered. It was three o'clock in the morning before he finished his inspection and reported that all the patches were undamaged and securely in place.

For ten days the salvage squad had been working without respite. All the time the German bombers kept flying over and attacking the *York*. The death of the divers was the climax. Knowing how badly the men needed rest, the salvage officer sent them ashore next day for a breather. He realized that a few hours in congenial surroundings away from bombing attacks would act like a tonic. In order to avoid a repetition of the tragedy he decided to carry out all future diving operations on the cruiser by night when the German pilots were off duty.

Returning to work on April 24, the salvage men made ready to get a pump into the engine room of the *York* to see if they could pump it out. The raiders flew over at intervals and gave them no rest. The harbor was alive with ships crammed with troops evacuated from Greece. The enemy pilots, reluctant to see them escape from their clutches, dived down with machine guns chattering to shoot up ships and troops. These attacks kept the salvage men busy going from ship to ship to plug the holes in their hulls.

About five-thirty in the afternoon another warning heralded the approach of a bomber whose stick of bombs straddled the *York*. When the explosion cleared it was seen that the submarine *Rover* moored beside the cruiser was badly damaged. This was a fatal blow, because the submarine was supplying all the light and power which Commander Wheeler needed to carry out his work. The explosion wrought such havoc in the *Rover* that she had to be towed inshore until she took the ground. With knocked-out batteries and holes in some of her tanks, she was of no further use to the salvage men.

At daybreak all energies were concentrated on discovering exactly what damage the *Rover* had sustained and testing her tanks. The salvage officer, however, would allow no diving work to be done until eight o'clock that night, when the *Protector* steamed in to moor beside the submarine. During the dark hours the diver fitted manhole plates which enabled some of the water to be pumped out and buoyancy to be regained. All next day leaks were sought and plugged, while the crew toiled at hand pumps to get rid of the water that leaked in. At night the salvage ship came back to allow the diver to examine the other side of the submarine. He found the tanks aft were so badly damaged that it was impossible to attempt repairs. The forward tanks were not so badly hit, so he took measurements of the damaged parts and withdrew at daybreak to get a little sleep.

On his return to the *Rover* that Sunday night of April 27, 1941, he learned that two wooden patches, suitably padded, had been constructed by the shipwrights, and during the dark hours he succeeded in fitting them over the leaking manholes and valves to stop the inflow.

What with one thing and another, the Fleet Salvage Officer had his hands full to overflowing. But he was too old a hand to be rattled by a surfeit of work. His job was to save ships, so he went round to the casualties as they occurred and gave his expert advice on how to put them right, never forgetting for an instant that his main task amid the slaughter of ships that was going on all round him was to lift the *York* and get her back into service. Imagine his profound disappointment when on the morning of April 28 he received a signal from headquarters to suspend salvage operations on the *York*. He was ordered to retrieve all the salvage plant and send the submarine *Rover* to Alexandria in tow of the salvage ship *Protector*.

At once the salvage men were switched to preparing the *Rover* for her voyage. They took out her gun and torpedoes to give her more stability, stowing them away carefully on the *Protector*, after which they loaded all the salvage gear from the *York*. They had done their best, but German air power had defeated them. At four o'clock on the afternoon of April 29 they moved slowly out of Suda Bay with the submarine in tow for Alexandria.

By that time the incessant raids had driven the crews of many ships into the hills for safety. The aircraft struck with little warning. Some men ran like rabbits. Others were demoralized when loud-speakers blared, and pandemonium broke loose as the guns roared and bombs exploded. The raids had so affected their nerves that they could stand it no longer. They were sitting targets, unable to hit back. To the German pilots it was all too easy. There was nothing to oppose them in the air, and after they had done their worst some of them showed their high spirits and contempt for the suffering they had inflicted by looping and rolling and flying on their backs and generally giving an exhibition of crazy flying that would have won the plaudits of the spectators at an air circus.

For another week Commander Wheeler dwelled among the falling bombs in order to give technical advice on the salvage of other ships. The cost of one of these wrecks, had it been expended a year or two earlier, would have provided a couple of salvage ships with trained crews that could have saved ships worth millions. The commander was awaiting an aircraft to take him to the steamer *Glengoyle* which was beached on the eastern side of Crete when the Walrus two-seater sent for him was shot down on the way. That was another nasty reminder of the risks they ran.

During those hectic days when the salvage officer gave attention to at least twenty ships while driving ahead with the work on the *York*, the King of Greece, the Crown Prince of Yugoslavia and other notabilities made their dramatic escape over the mountains of Greece to the safety of Crete. Among this august company Commander Wheeler stayed in the same hotel in Canea to snatch what sleep he could. And it was with the King of Greece, the Crown Prince of Yugoslavia, and their retinues, on Wednesday, May 7, 1941, that he embarked in the Sunderland flying boat that was to take them into exile.

The flying boat was crowded with about seventy people. Apart from the crew, Commander Wheeler was the only Englishman among them. As the Sunderland's engines mounted to a roar and she gathered speed to take off from the waters of Suda Bay, the King of Greece glanced back at the beloved land which he was not to see again for many years.

At that moment Commander Wheeler's thoughts and eyes were fixed on the wreck of H.M.S. *York*. The divers had given their lives for her. All their sacrifices were vain. The consummate skill of the devoted salvage men was wasted, their toil counted for nought. Yet in two more days he could have saved her — if!

CHAPTER IX

A Graveyard of Wrecks

THE growth of the Italian Air Force wrought a profound strategical change in the Mediterranean, for it rendered Malta untenable by the Royal Navy. The British naval base, which had hitherto dominated the middle Mediterranean, was endangered by air power. Recognizing this, the Admiralty with commendable prudence and foresight removed the headquarters and main elements of the Mediterranean fleet to Alexandria to protect the ships from a lightning attack by hostile bombers.

The consequence was that when Mussolini saw the British Army pushed into the sea at Dunkirk and decided to throw in his lot with Hitler on June 10, 1940, Malta lay wide open to air attack. One of the most strongly fortified islands in the world, it was vulnerable from the air. The guns of the forts, sited to destroy ships, were of little use against enemy bombers. Lacking antiaircraft batteries of high-angle guns and fighter aircraft, the island was practically defenseless. Great Britain was almost in as sad a plight. By a miracle of seamanship she had saved her army from Dunkirk, but it was an army without arms. All that vast equipment, so slowly built up at great cost, was lost.

A bare sixty miles away from Malta lay Sicily, its airfields crammed with Italian aircraft. The Italian airmen, taking an early morning flip before breakfast, could scatter a few bombs over Malta as an appetizer for the coffee and rolls that awaited their return, just as the simple Englishman in good old days could stroll along the seafront to acquire an appetite for the ham and eggs. There was not a single fighter aircraft in the island. The Royal Air Force had a few men stationed there with two or three flying boats, and that was all.

Down in the dock warehouses were four Gladiators, all carefully packed in crates, waiting for a ship to carry them on to the navy at Alexandria. The flying-boat pilots unpacked and assembled the Gladiators without ado. Although they had never before flown a fighter aircraft, they quickly mastered the controls and gave the Italians a nasty shock. One of the Gladiators met trouble at any early date, but the other three won such a warm place in the hearts of the Maltese that they named them Faith, Hope, and Charity.

No odds were too great for the courgeous flying-boat pilots. They attacked fifty or sixty enemy aircraft with as much zest as they attacked half a dozen. Day after day for three months the lone Gladiators fought the Italians in sortie after sortie until a few Hurricanes could be spared to help them. These, with other British aircraft flown off carriers, gradually built up the defenses of the island.

With Sicilian airfields dominating the Sicilian Channel through which all sea traffic had to pass to the Middle East, it was suicidal for an Allied ship to attempt the passage. And because Malta, in turn, dominated the shipping lanes to North Africa, it was vital for Italy to subdue the island.

As the bombing attacks grew in intensity and the historic old buildings were destroyed, the Maltese worked with a will cutting shelters in the limestone of which the island is composed. Great tunnels and passages had in past ages been driven through the rock as underground communications between fort and fort. These, which provided shelter for thousands, were enlarged; many more were hacked out by the inhabitants with picks forged in the naval workshops. Deep in the limestone crags, the Royal Engineers carved great caverns with their pneumatic drills until there was a refuge for all.

The Maltese helped to man the guns, they chipped away to

enlarge the shelters in the limestone, they toiled to clear the mounds of rubble obstructing the streets and, in between times, contrived to grow what crops they could in the little stone-walled fields dotting their craggy island.

Cut off from the normal sources of supply, they started to feel the pinch. Essentials such as food, aviation fuel, and munitions, which began to run short, could be replenished only by convoys of ships that were forced to fight their way through, with bitter losses.

The enemy paid the price. Naval gunners on the ships and aircraft from the carriers shot down dozens of bombers into the sea. From the day that Italy loosed her attack on the impregnable little island until New Year's Day of 1942 the gunners of Malta destroyed 236 enemy aircraft while British fighter pilots destroyed 893 enemy fighters and bombers against their own losses of 568.

By then, British bombers from Malta were hitting the Italian mainland, British submarines were sinking the ships laden with supplies for Rommel's army in North Africa. The German and Italian bombers poured thousands of tons of bombs upon Malta in the early months of 1942. Valletta lay in ruins. Wrecks cluttered the harbor. The Maltese were living like troglodytes in their limestone caves, yet their battered little island proved such a menace to the sea lines of Rommel that the German and Italian commands were constrained to make a final frantic effort to wipe it off the map. Wave after wave of bombers flew over to do the worst. The island was under attack all round the clock. The bombing reached its climax about the middle of April and then dwindled as the month wore on.

Supplies which had run the gantlet in March were nearing exhaustion. Ammunition was getting so short that the gunners had to be rationed. The stocks of aviation fuel became so low that the dire need of the Royal Air Force led Admiral Cunningham to send gas by submarine to insure that it reached the island in time to keep the fighter pilots flying. The only instructions to the submarine commander were to avoid trouble and get there. And it was in this submarine, the *Porpoise*, with salvage pumps lashed to her decks and the pipes and gear stowed inside her, that Commander G. J. Wheeler went to see what could be done to get one or two docks in Malta working again in time for the next convoy. The approach of the submerged *Porpoise* to the south side of the island was unseen by the enemy, but the persistent air raids followed each other so closely that she was forced to lurk on the bottom all day before she was able to slink into port at dusk.

Valletta harbor was a slaughterhouse of ships. Wrecks were everywhere. Sunken lighters and canal craft obstructed the wharves; the *Pampas* lay with a broken back in the middle of the Marsa after having burned for days; the *Talabot*, hit by bombs and blown up by her own depth charges, lay not far off; the submarine *Glaucus* was lying broken in half in about forty feet of water blocking the entrance of a dry dock; the submarine *Pandora* had rolled over with a dozen torpedoes on board and was just showing her conning tower above the surface. One ship lay on her side in pieces, another sat up on her stern with her bow right across the top of a dry dock. French Creek was a graveyard of ships large and small. Kalkara Creek contained five big wrecks. Everywhere were trawlers, lighters, submarines, drifters, sweepers, all the little craft that were wont to work the harbor, the warships that guarded it, and the merchant ships that had served it for the last time.

Malta in those April days of 1942 was a terrible example of air power. The wharves were so choked with wrecks that no ship could get alongside to unload. The fantastic piles of debris on the roads prevented any vehicle from reaching the wharves to carry cargo away. The havoc would take years to repair.

The salvage officer was appalled at the scene of destruction. The Maltese could still call up a smile, but the grimness of life was rammed home to him when men with whom he had chatted a few hours previously were wiped out by blast or buried under bombed buildings. Moving round in that desolation, he selected the wharves and quays that might be cleared, the wrecks across which platforms might be built to allow ships to unload beside them. He stressed the urgency of keeping the two or three surviving tugs and small craft in service and asked for several light pumps to be sent from Alexandria by submarine. Strangely enough, where newer ships were sunk all over the place, there was one old landing craft which was used in the Dardanelles in the First World War that still remained afloat in defiance of the worst the enemy could do.

Methodically the salvage officer compiled his long list of wrecks and advised what was to be done with them, all too frequently adding the words "total loss" or "case for demolition."

There was the mighty floating dock rent in three, lying on the bottom off Magazine Wharf: never again would it rise gently under the keel of a proud battleship to lift her bodily into the air so that she could be examined and repaired.

A mile offshore in sixty feet of water H.M.S. *Breconshire* was lying with a little of her starboard bilge showing above the surface. Men were still working to remove as much of the fuel oil from her tanks as they could extract through a hole cut in her side. Already they had recovered eight hundred tons. Studying her, the salvage officer reported that he was doubtful if she could ever be turned upright again and that salvage operations would definitely take some months.

A big ship of 9600 tons, H.M.S. *Breconshire* was rather an oddity, inasmuch as the bow part of her was constructed as an oil tanker while the after part was designed for carrying general cargo. The Glen Line built her as an all-purpose ship, and when she was requisitioned by the Admiralty her dual capacity was of such importance that she was put on the Malta run. Sometimes she sailed from Alexandria in convoy, more often she sailed alone; but whenever she arrived at Valletta she was doubly welcome because she always replenished the supplies that were most wanted.

She had speed, she had first-class guns and gunners, and her commander, Captain C. A. G. Hutchinson, D.S.O., R.N., was an adept at dodging bombs. Watching the attackers until he saw the bombs fall away, he used to alter course just at the right moment to make the missiles fall wide. The gunners of the *Breconshire* saw many of their kills fall flaming into the sea. For their part, the Italian and German pilots, seeing the ship enveloped in clouds of spray as their bombs exploded, more than once claimed to have sent her to the bottom. They loved her no more than she loved them and it was always war between them.

She was one of four ships to leave Alexandria on March 20, 1942, in an attempt to run supplies through to Malta. Two days later their escort of light cruisers and destroyers attacked an Italian naval force of overwhelming strength and sent an enemy battleship with its screen of cruisers and destroyers scuttling for safety while the four supply ships fought off the German bombers and escaped in a smoke screen to make their diverse ways to the island. All four ships perished. One was sunk a few miles off Malta and two were sunk after reaching harbor. The *Breconshire* herself survived all perils until she was about five miles offshore when a lone German raider, flying close to the surface, came sneaking out of the early morning haze. The *Breconshire*'s gunners did their best, but the enemy pilot gave them no chance. A bomb hit the ship in the engine room and stopped her in her tracks.

Her call for help soon brought H.M.S. *Penelope* to try to tow her in. She was big and unmanageable and gave some trouble in getting the towing wire fixed. When coupled up, the *Breconshire* could make no more than about 600 yards in the first hour. The *Penelope* hung on desperately. In five hours she towed the cripple about two miles nearer safety; and it took exactly eleven hours to haul the *Breconshire* four miles into the shelter of Marsa Scirrocco, where she took ground at the side of the channel about a mile offshore. She was full of the things the island needed. Her tanks were loaded with oil, her holds with munitions. The enemy knew they had hit her and were determined to destroy her. For two days she was harried by enemy aircraft. Her gunners fought zealously to save her, but one or two more direct hits set her ablaze and soon after being abandoned she heeled over and sank just before noon on March 27, 1942. It was due to her masts and funnels hitting the bottom that she was checked from swinging right over and turning upside down.

As for H.M.S. *Penelope*, when Commander Wheeler saw her sitting beside the dock she was so full of holes that her crew had rechristened her H.M.S. *Pepperpot*. Yet her men remained cheery and her guns could still shoot despite the damage she had suffered. Everyone in the dockyard who could lend a hand played a part in plugging and patching the countless holes. She looked an extraordinary sight with plugs of wood sprouting out of her hull all over the place as though she were suffering from some eruption.

There was considerable excitement in Valletta the night the *Penelope* raised steam and crept quietly out of harbor on her way to Gibraltar. No one thought she could survive the voyage, but she limped back to the Rock safely, leaving behind her the overturned *Breconshire* peeping out of the Mediterranean like a stranded whale.

There the *Breconshire* lay when a salvage officer from the Admiralty, Captain O. T. Harrison, took the salvage ship *Sea Salvor* with eight divers out to Malta after the war to see what was to be done with her. Being an obstruction, it was essential to remove her. The question was how to do it. In the end the decision was taken to refloat her bottom up.

This miracle was first performed after the First World War by the Italians who lifted out the guns and cut off the turrets of the upside-down battleship *Leonardo da Vinci*, pumped compressed air into her as though they were blowing up an automobile tire and floated her to the surface. Towing her to dry dock for repairs, they completed the miracle by taking her to sea and turning her right side up again. I watched more than one of the German warships scuttled in Scapa Flow being refloated in the same way.

Backed by the knowledge and experience derived from past cases, it was proposed to perform the miracle again. The technical difficulties remained formidable. Differences in ships pose different problems. The size of a ship, the position of the engine room, strength of bulkheads, extent and position of the damage are all important factors that tend to complicate the general problem.

Leaving nothing to chance, the salvage officer ordered an exact model of the *Breconshire* to be constructed. This model, twelve feet long, had every bulkhead, valve, and fitting duplicated in miniature, according to the original plans of the wreck. Fortunately there was on the island a naval experimental tank in which the technical officers of the navy had been in the habit of making their tests. In this the salvage officer carried out his experiments. Sinking the model on the bottom at the same angle as the *Breconshire*, he pumped air into her fore and aft to note what happened, then he jotted down his calculations. This compartment made tight down to a certain level would give him so much buoyancy to lift so many tons, that compartment made airtight would lift so many more tons, and if he could make enough compartments airtight to give him sufficient buoyancy to lift the whole weight of the ship he knew he could refloat her.

It was, of course, important that the buoyancy should be in the right places, otherwise the wreck might overbalance and in a few moments spill out all the air that the salvors had pumped into her in the previous three or four days. I have seen the bow of a sunken battleship swing up spouting cascades of water high into the heavens owing to the compressed air gushing out of her because she was not properly balanced.

To achieve this perfect balance is another problem which the salvage officer has to solve. The greater the weight to be lifted, the greater the air pressure. If a pressure of say seven pounds to the square inch is sufficient to lift the bow, which is light, it will need a bigger pressure to lift the stern which is heavy with the weight of the engines. It is therefore important that all outlets leading from one compartment to another are carefully stopped, otherwise the air in the lower part of the ship will make its way to the higher part of the ship and push it up until the air can escape from underneath and gush to the surface.

These were a few of the problems which the salvage officer had to study and solve with his model in the tank. When at length he had completed his calculations, he felt sure he could refloat the wreck bottom up.

Putting the divers to work with their underwater cutters, he ordered them to cut off the mast and bridge and funnel. All this had to be sheared off so that nothing would stop the wreck from turning bottom up when the time was ripe. Even a trifling obstruction might have interfered with operations. I once observed two powerful tugs brought to a standstill by a jagged piece of plate which hung from a wreck and fouled the sea bed. They might have been trying to tow a mountain for all the impression they made, and before they could go on the obstruction had to be cleared.

Working with a will, the divers gradually burned through all the top-hamper of the ship until they had cleared the decks of seven hundred tons of metal. They could work all right so long as they were standing on the sea bed. Their troubles started when they went inside the ship. All the decks and ceilings which ought to have been flat were sloping at an acute angle, and the difficulty of moving about in a diving suit hampered by the air pipe can be imagined. The flooding valves of the ship were unfortunately open, and they had to be closed to make the compartments tight. The one way to get at them was through a small tunnel in which it was impossible to turn, so the diver had to wriggle in feet foremost to get to the valves and make his way out head first.

Here was another case where fuel oil smothered everything and cut off all light. Toiling like blind men by touch did not make the work of the divers any easier. The oil was such a nuisance that sometimes they discarded their diving suits and went down naked, breathing through a respirator attached to a tube that went to the surface.

Anxious to push on with the job, they often exceeded the recognized diving spells under water and worked for as long as five hours on end. Then to avoid an attack of diver's paralysis or bends, caused by the excess of nitrogen in the blood due to breathing air under pressure, they had to spend up to six hours in the recompression chamber to allow the nitrogen to pass off without harmful effects.

The oil in the tanks was an ever-present danger when the divers were using their flaming cutters. Not infrequently the oil ignited and caused a flashback in the cutter. Threatened by fire forward, they braved the possibility of explosions aft, for the stern holds were full of bombs and various munitions. What might have transpired if they had accidentally touched off something with their torches does not bear thinking about. The risk was there, but they took it in their stride without fuss.

They found that five plates had been blown out of the hull. Before she could be refloated this hole had to be made good. Normally it would have necessitated a large patch. Exploring the sea bed round the wreck, the divers came on the missing plates. Buckled though they were, this did not worry the salvage men. Sending the plates to the surface, the salvors took them ashore to be heated and rolled out again in the dockyard.

Then the plates were refitted on the hull of the ship and bolted home. It saved a lot of time and trouble. For months the divers busied themselves about the wreck, stopping up all the vents in the hull to make the bottom and sides airtight. One by one they fitted air connections into the tanks and various compartments. So many were needed that they could not find enough air valves in the island to do the job. Then someone had the brilliant notion of using ordinary water faucets. They served the purpose excellently. By the time the divers were finished they had fitted about forty air connections to be linked up with the air lines when the big test came.

There was much speculation in Malta as to whether the plan would succeed, but the salvors themselves had no doubt about it. For four months they had struggled with difficulty after difficulty to complete the work. On August 7, 1950, the various air connections were linked up with the air compressors on three salvage ships, the *Sea Salvor*, the *Retrieve* and the *Dispenser*. The air compressors were started and kept working steadily until next day, when the weather turned bad and the seas broke away some of the air lines. When they were connected again, the compressors continued their monotonous song, until a certain liveliness in the bow told the salvors that they were regaining buoyancy.

Next morning the bow pushed above the surface as planned. The massive weight in the afterpart still kept the stern anchored to the sea bed; but as the bow lifted, it slowly eased the weight off the stern and enabled the wreck to pivot inch by inch until it was nearly bottom up. The completion of this turning movement enabled the salvage officer to switch the air compressors to the after-holds. Now and again a compressor had to be stopped for some oil and a few adjustments, or a diver dropped down to make sure that all was going well. Hour by hour as the compressed air squeezed the water down in her holds, the stern grew more buoyant, until a week after the compressors were started the ship rose to the surface and floated bottom up among the salvage craft.

The *Breconshire* showed not the slightest tendency to overturn. The divers had made her hull so airtight that she lost hardly any air. It had been officially decided that after being refloated she should be towed out to sea and sunk in deep water. But now that she was safely afloat it was recognized that she was worth something as scrap metal — if anyone could be induced to buy her.

A private firm in Malta was quick to seize the chance. Assuring themselves that she would keep afloat as long as they maintained the air pressure, and that she was well-balanced with the center of gravity low enough to obviate the danger of overturning, they bought her and eventually she was towed to Genoa to be broken up.

In stating that it would take months to salve her and that it was doubtful if she could ever be uprighted again, the judgment delivered eight years earlier by Commander Wheeler was at last confirmed.

CHAPTER X

Raising a Floating Dock

IN those blessed days before the enemy reduced Valletta to mounds of rubble and filled the harbors and creeks with wrecks, the frontage of Laboratory Wharf and Magazine Wharf was mainly occupied by the Admiralty floating dock. A floating dock is by no means a thing of beauty, though I have on occasions seen one in certain atmospheric conditions which appeared as a dream of loveliness when compared with many modernistic paintings and sculptures. It is a steel structure designed for the strictly utilitarian purpose of sinking down in the sea to enable a battleship or any other ship to float into it, and then rising under the keel to lift the ship bodily out of the water until the floor or deck of the floating dock becomes high and dry enough to enable men to do necessary repairs to the hull or propellers of the ship.

That man can lift a mighty ship weighing thirty or forty thousand tons bodily out of the sea is nevertheless a miracle, notwithstanding that millions who read about it regard it as commonplace and fail to recognize the wonder of it. The miracle is worked, of course, by building up the walls and floor of the dock on a series of tanks which can be filled with water to sink the structure to the required depth and pumped out again to bring the dock to the surface with the ship cradled safely on the keel blocks between the two steel walls. In such simple ways do the naval constructors and engineers achieve their wonders. All that is visible of a floating dock is bare and ugly; its invisible part is a veritable honeycomb of enormous tanks, all connected by pipes with the pumping machinery in the side walls.

The floating dock at Malta was 960 feet long and 180 feet broad and its outer walls were 70 feet deep. It was a vast structure which provided a bombing target for the enemy that could not be missed. The Italian bombers attacked it in 1940 with such celerity and accuracy that the floating dock floated no longer, but lay a broken wreck on the bottom of Grand Harbor.

When the Fleet Salvage Officer arrived by submarine from Alexandria in April 1942, to see what could be done to provide unloading facilities in Malta for the next convoy, the sunken dock had been on the bottom for over a year. There was nothing he could do about it except leave it alone. His mission concerned more urgent matters that meant life or death to the Maltese, the landing of food and fuel and ammunition from any of the ships in the approaching convoy that came through safely.

Throughout the rest of the war the bombs rained from the sky over Grand Harbor. The dock was unmoved. The currents played about it, the barnacles multiplied on its steel walls and the little fishes fed among the sea growths that anchored themselves to the plates.

With the defeat of the enemy came the task of rebuilding Malta and restoring its dock and harbor facilities. The raising of the floating dock was one of the problems confronting the naval authorities. A floating dock in Malta harbor was essential for the overhaul of warships in times of peace, and before a new floating dock could be moored off the old site it was necessary to get the broken dock out of the way.

It would be an understatement to call the dock anything less than gigantic. The side walls of the dock measured seventy feet exactly from top to bottom. A terrace of thirty-two houses each with a frontage of thirty feet could be built along each of its sides which stretched for nearly a fifth of a mile.

To raise this colossal structure was the problem which the

experts faced. Whereas it was easy enough to raise and lower it by filling and pumping water out of its tanks when it was intact, the question of lifting it in its fractured condition was much more baffling. The only way to make sure of refloating the dock was to build models with which to experiment in order to see what happened.

Meanwhile, divers were set to work on the job of cutting the dock into three sections. The bombs had already gone far towards performing this feat, but the parts were not actually separated. They were held together by great lengths of crumpled plates. For months the divers ate through these plates with their flaming torches, melting their way inch by inch through the steel until by the end of 1947 the walls of the dock were cut away from the central floor or deck of the structure. Thus the preliminary operation in the raising of the dock was finished.

While the divers were carrying out their unseen work under water, the naval constructors were not idle. Working to the plans of the dock, they had models constructed in the workshop to duplicate in miniature the features of the giant.

Boys the world over would have loved to join in the games that the experts played with these models. Not that the experts regarded them as games. To the specialists they were serious scientific experiments designed to furnish the information which would enable them to remove the three sections of the sunken dock. Still, the average man and woman might have been forgiven — had they come across the experts bending over the experimental tank watching the behavior of the models — for thinking that some men have queer ways of amusing themselves.

One wall of the dock was known as the northeast section and the other as the southwest section, to prevent any misunderstandings in official quarters about the part of the dock which was being dealt with. Constructor W. G. John and Commander W. R. Fell, who were given the important work of removing the dock, were joined early in August 1948 by a naval constructor from England, Mr. W. R. Seward. The most precious part of Mr. Seward's luggage was a model of the southwest portion of the dock. It was a beautiful model that gleamed like gold. Though made of brass, it was almost as precious as gold, for it was designed to save as much public money as possible in carrying out the salvage work. In this exquisite little model all the damage wrought by the bombs in the walls of the various tanks, as well as all the damage arising from rust and decay, was faithfully reproduced. The little tanks had their tiny pipes which would enable the water to be blown out of various tanks as desired by the experts.

Although the most desirable method of removing the dock was to refloat each section and tow it away, it was by no means certain that this could be done. There was indeed the possibility that in the last resort the dock might have to be cut up by divers with their underwater cutters and removed piecemeal. The extreme difficulty of the problem forced the experts to consider this possibility as well as the prospect of demolishing the dock with explosives.

Mr. Seward's model was designed to clinch the matter and remove all uncertainty. Accompanying Captain John and Commander Fell to the naval experimental tank lying behind Laboratory Wharf at the foot of the Corradino Heights, Mr. Seward took his model and sank it to the bottom of the tank. Numerous experiments followed in which various tanks in the model were blown out to define how much buoyancy would have to be obtained to raise the structure in one piece, and which tanks would have to be freed of water to insure sufficient stability. Time and again the experts gathered round the naval tank to observe how the model behaved under different conditions. The model tilted this way and that as it came to the surface. By the time they had worked out which tanks would have to be emptied to obtain the necessary buoyancy, they had confirmed their hope that it would be possible to refloat the section whole instead of going to the endless trouble of cutting it up and hauling it away in pieces. Gratified by their experiments, the salvors decided to lift an end of the northeast section as a preliminary test for working out the general plan. The pumping out of the key tanks was put in hand. By August 27 the experts saw one end of the dock rise to the surface. This was just what they wanted. It provided them with an opportunity of making a careful survey of the tanks. The divers surveyed the tanks with meticulous care and their report was heartening. Judging by what they had seen, the experts had been expecting considerable damage, instead of which it was much lighter than they anticipated. In view of this favorable evidence, they concluded that it would be possible to make good one tank after another all down the starboard side of the section and win the major part of the buoyancy required. Jotting down his figures, Mr. Seward calculated that the clearance of these tanks would bring the section up with a heavy list to port. Having assured himself that the sections could be refloated whole, he left the men on the spot to get on with the job.

The divers were set to work on the tanks, patching and plugging and making them watertight so that they could be pumped out. They drove ahead until by September 28 they had patched the first series of tanks. When these were pumped out, the wall of the dock came up and floated with a heavy list exactly as predicted.

A part of it was so badly damaged by bombs that it remained submerged. Until this part was raised it was impossible to tow the section away. A cofferdam was accordingly built round this damaged part to allow it to be pumped out. This not only brought the whole section on a more even keel and corrected the list in the lengthy wall of the dock, but it was now possible for the divers to repair ten more tanks which sufficed to refloat the entire section. On October 15 the tugs took charge of it and towed it across Grand Harbor to park it on a nearby beach.

On the same day some of the tanks of the southwest section were blown out by compressed air to bring one end above the surface. The salvors were far from happy about it. This was not the first time it had been tackled. In earlier attempts, one of the walls had been cut by the divers and this was now a source of weakness. The bombs had also wrought much more damage than in the other section, with the result that there was grave risk of the section breaking in two if it were strained unduly. The salvors had no desire to take two bites at the cherry; their one desire was to finish it all at once and be done with it.

The walls had already buckled under previous unsuccessful attempts to raise it. Now that one end was afloat and the other resting on the bottom without support for the intervening portion, the buckling of the wall plates began to increase under the strain. The experts examined the weak spots anxiously. Next day the fractures had grown perceptibly longer, and by October 13 a third of the section came to rest on the bottom while the other portion rose at an angle which brought the end of it ten feet clear of the surface. The section was broken right across the bottom plates and was merely held together by the upper plating.

The position was desperate. Unless something were done to ease the strain the section would break in two and complicate a problem that was already complicated enough. In the circumstances the salvors were driven to rely on a desperate remedy — to try to refloat the sunken part of the dock quickly in order to prevent the upper walls from being torn apart. Luck was with them. They found that two tanks in the sunken portion were intact and that they could be blown out by compressed air.

They forced the water out of the tanks. For a moment

nothing happened. The salvors looked on dubiously, they were very uneasy in their minds. Then the sunken portion of the dock came unstuck from the sea bed and shot to the surface, flinging cascades of water and mud and wreckage high into the air. It was an astonishing spectacle. When the disturbance died down the two extreme ends of the dock were jutting at an angle right out of the water while the point where they joined was well below the surface. Shifting their pumps to the submerged portion, the salvage men pumped away until the whole section was afloat.

Both ends were free except for a few plates which held them together. The severed plates ground and worked about in an alarming manner. Fortunately the surface of the sea was unruffled, but in spite of the calm conditions the experts had an anxious time until the section was towed away and safely beached.

With the two great walls of the dock out of the way, it might be imagined that the worst was over. Far from it. The flat central section which promised to be a simple straightforward job turned out to be unexpectedly difficult because of a belt of air.

It was not possible to spare the divers to examine the central section until the side sections were out of the way. When the divers came to make their survey they discovered that a belt of air had been trapped at the top of the tanks, otherwise under the floor, or deck, of the dock, and had wrought havoc with the steel plates. There were no vents in the deck to enable the air to escape. For six or seven years the air and the salt water had combined to corrode the plates until in some places it had eaten away gaps up to eighteen inches deep. This damage would not have occurred if the plates had been immersed in the sea, for they would have remained uncorroded and as strong as when they sank.

The only thing to be done was to patch tank after tank, which the divers did, until one end of the section was re-

floated. Transferring operations to the other end of the section, the divers connected a battery of air compressors to
three of the tanks which, when they were blown out, lifted
that end of the dock for forty feet. As the dock came up,
the compressed air gushed out of the holes in the lower parts
of the tanks, blowing cascades of water high in the air. For
a while the section was fully afloat, then as the air escaped it
sank again.

There was but one way to overcome the difficulty — to
patch the holes through which the air escaped. Relays of
divers thereupon worked on the job night and day for the
next fortnight, and on December 8 a further test was made.
For an hour or two the section floated with the sea boiling
around it as the air escaped. Then as it lost buoyancy it slowly
sank for the second time.

Once more the divers were sent down to extend their patching operations to other compartments. They toiled away until
the salvage experts were convinced that the section could play
them no further tricks. On December 21, 1948, they started
up the compressors again. It was third time lucky. The great
floor of the dock emerged from the sea bed and was towed
away to the beaching ground to be scrapped.

CHAPTER XI

New Patch Work

T HE mention of patch work calls up visions of the patch-work quilts of Victorian times with their multicolored pieces stretched across beds like gigantic jigsaw puzzles. It is, however, with another kind of patch work that the salvage man has to deal, the patch work that saves ships. In bygone days, when ships were built on a smaller scale, all sorts of things were used to stop up holes after a collision, including tarpaulins and mattresses, until the ship's carpenter could construct a more durable patch. Emergency methods were therefore inclined to be rather haphazard.

But the First World War produced so many casualties from mine and torpedo that patching began to assume something of a science. The suggestion that a ship might be patched with concrete would have been laughed at by shipmasters in 1914, but before the end of that war the broken halves of the steamship *Araby* had been salved by building two walls of concrete across them, while a torpedoed steamer had been repaired by patching the hole in her hull with concrete to prove that concrete patches were feasible. The ship was duly certified as seaworthy, and today the use of concrete in salving ships is so commonplace that it arouses no comment in salvage circles.

It was the lack of a dry dock in which to dock the torpedoed P. & O. liner *Berrima* in March 1917 that gave Commander G. J. Wheeler the brilliant idea of building a gigantic wooden patch weighing forty-two tons in three sections on the quayside and patching the *Berrima* while she remained afloat. Nothing like it had ever been attempted before, and that huge patch was the forerunner of the so-called standard patch.

Concrete patches and large wooden patches were thus a normal part of marine salvage practice when the Second World War broke out and there seemed little likelihood of further developments so far as patches were concerned. Unlikely as it seemed, however, new developments in the patching of ships did occur as the war progressed. The first, due to Commander Wheeler, undoubtedly sprang directly from the big patch he had constructed for the *Berrima* nearly twenty-five years earlier.

In the days of November 1941, with British forces besieged in Tobruk and Rommel hoping to break through to Cairo, the only way of getting supplies to the beleaguered troops was by sea. It was rough going — with enemy submarines lurking at periscope depth to let loose their torpedoes and enemy bombers doing their worst from the air. Our ships suffered many casualties while making that passage along the coast, with the result that a few salvage men were installed at Tobruk to render first aid and help them on their way out of the danger zone.

Commander Wheeler, who went along to Tobruk, was cut off like the rest from the usual amenities. The troops were used to sand in their hair, in their eyes, and in their food. If the bully beef was a bit rough to the palate now and again, it was better that way than no beef at all. The salvage officer was warmly welcomed in several mess tents. The messes had not yet attained the refinements of the best restaurants, though there were boxes to sit on and a couple of big boxes upended to serve as a bar in most. Two sardines on toast tainted with paraffin from the primus stove could generally be relied upon as a fish course, followed by the usual bully beef. To cut off a chunk of beef with a fishy knife was considered the worst of form, so to avoid tainting the beef with sardines it was the custom to break off a piece with the fingers.

After these wartime picnics, it was something of a shock when the salvage officer sat down on the salvage-depot ship at a table covered with a snow-white tablecloth and provided with spotless napkins. He was so startled that he almost committed the unforgivable sin of asking where they came from, but fortunately second thoughts prevailed and the meal proceeded unruffled by awkward questions.

He was in Tobruk on his lawful occasions when H.M.S. *Glenroy* was attacked from the air between Mersa Matruh and Tobruk and hit by a torpedo from an aircraft. Troops and sailors on board were promptly transferred to the destroyer *Ferndale* and taken on to Tobruk while H.M.S. *Carlisle* started to tow the *Glenroy* back to Alexandria.

She was hit about four o'clock on the Sunday afternoon of November 23, 1941, and the captain at once sought to discover her injuries. A hole of unknown size in her hull opened a tank to the sea, a flooded engine room came from a damaged bulkhead, other leaks started to flood some of the holds. The stricken ship moved along slowly all through the night. As is to be expected, she was very sluggish. The weight of water seeping into her was gradually dragging her down by the stern. Meanwhile those on board strove to stop the leaks and shore up weakened bulkheads while the *Carlisle* hung on grimly in the hope of bringing her back to Alexandria.

The fates were against them. It became obvious next day that the only chance of saving her was to put her ashore. Eventually she was grounded about a mile from Mersa Matruh.

An urgent call the following day to Commander Wheeler instructed him to proceed to her assistance. Accordingly he boarded a motor launch and started on the 190-mile sea voyage to Mersa Matruh. The sea was rough, the launch's motors had the devil in them, for when one worked the other jibbed, and only occasionally would they turn over in unison. The little craft slogged along, pushing her nose into the seas, while Commander Wheeler made the best of things, as seamen always do. Leaving Tobruk about six o'clock in the evening of November 23, the motor boat took until three o'clock the next afternoon to cover those 190 miles. It was a marked contrast to his rush at forty knots, a week or two later, to get two or three bombed ships away from Tobruk.

On his arrival, the salvage officer found the *Glenroy* beached astern with her bow afloat. Luckily a tug had arrived with pumps from Alexandria. There was intense activity for a few hours installing three pumps while bulkheads were strengthened and leaks stopped. Then with pumps running sweetly she slid off into deep water just after ten o'clock that night. A few more strenuous hours were spent in making her safe for the voyage, and just after three o'clock in the morning the tug started to tow her to Alexandria.

Thankful for a few dark hours to cover her movements, the salvage officer guessed that the enemy, having winged her, would not let her make the voyage back without interference. He was right.

Marking the *Glenroy* snailing along behind the tug, they soon sent their bombers to attack her. The gunners did their best to blow the planes out of the sky while the planes were just as intent to send the *Glenroy*, with the tug, to the bottom. Evasive action at two or three knots with a sinking ship in tow was impossible. The only thing for the tug to do was to steer straight ahead and hope for the best. In due course another tug came along to help to tow the *Glenroy* home. With enemy bombers concentrating on the *Glenroy* and her guns concentrating on the bombers, the position of those on board was not enviable. They were shaken from time to time with near misses, the *Glenroy* received further damage, and how she managed to survive until darkness fell was something of a mystery.

The tugs steamed ahead at their best gait during the night. The pumps on the *Glenroy* poured out water without ceasing. They just managed to hold their own.

Daylight brought another day of peril. The men knew not when the bombers would appear. Every hour the procession crawled two or three miles nearer to safety. Thanks to the superb shooting of the gunners, they managed to survive and keep afloat until nightfall.

The dawn of the next day found them nearing home. They were close enough to Alexandria to make it unwise for the enemy bombers to run the risk of the British fighters. Throughout the day the *Glenroy* strained at the towing cable as the tugs forged ahead. By ten o'clock on the night of November 29 their ordeal was over. It took them fifty-five hours to cover a hundred and fifty miles — an average speed of three miles an hour — during which they endured fifteen separate attacks from the air.

The men, dropping with fatigue, were asleep almost before they could turn in. When they awakened, it was to fresh trouble. The channel into the port was but thirty-five feet deep and the *Glenroy* was drawing thirty-eight feet aft. To attempt to take her in would have blocked the channel. Accordingly they decided to try to tip her, to alter her trim by shifting weight from her stern and pumping water into her forward tanks. As they anticipated, her stern came up and her bow went down to give them just enough clearance under her keel to use the channel.

Before they could tow her into harbor a gale sprang up. For three days she rode it out, while pumps kept the water down, and as soon as the gale abated they maneuvered her into the harbor. By eight o'clock on the morning of December 4 she was safely moored.

All that remained to be done was to get her into dry dock for repairs. As the dock would not be vacant until December 10, the crew ran the pumps occasionally to control the water

and got the diver to survey the damage while they were waiting to dock her. A star-shaped hole twenty-five feet high and
twenty-five feet wide with buckled plates around it summed
up the damage which the diver found. This had to be patched
to make the *Glenroy* seaworthy again.

By the time December 10 arrived, the *Glenroy* was obliged
to give precedence to another ship that was in a more parlous
state. Her entry into dry dock was therefore postponed until
December 19.

That day dawned with the dramatic sinking of the *Queen
Elizabeth* and *Valiant* by Italian charioteers. Of necessity,
the *Valiant* had first claim on the dry dock, which she
would certainly occupy for three months to come. Thus for
the second time the *Glenroy* was cheated out of her turn to
dry dock and was forced to remain at her moorings in the
harbor.

It was a similar situation which Commander Wheeler had
faced in 1917 — a torpedoed ship with an immense hole and
no dry dock available for repairing her. He knew quite well
that what he had done before he could do again, consequently
he decided to overcome the difficulty on the same broad lines
as before by having a patch built on the quayside and fixing
it in place while the *Glenroy* remained afloat. Being unable to
find balks of timber long enough for his purpose in the dockyard, he discarded the idea of a wooden patch and got the
dockyard to make an immense steel patch forty-one feet long
by twenty-seven feet deep in two sections.

With all the resources of the dockyard concentrated on the
damaged *Queen Elizabeth* and *Valiant*, delay in dealing with
the *Glenroy* was to be expected. By January 30, however,
the first section of the patch was bolted home by the divers
after they had cut away the ragged plates that were obstruc-
tive. On February 24 the floating crane swung into position
the upper part of the patch upon which the divers toiled until
March 9 before securing the last bolt. It is interesting to record

that they drilled holes in the steel plates of the *Glenroy* for 750 bolts, so it can be imagined how onerous was their work. An Italian prisoner of war showed them how to marry the edges of the steel patch to the hull by a new method of underwater welding.

To make sure that his patch would not give way under heavy seas, Commander Wheeler shored it inside with balks of timber and strengthened it with various steel fitments to wed it to the hull, after which a great box was built in the holds to overlap the patch. This box, filled with seventy tons of concrete, made a big concrete wall six feet wide at the bottom and four feet wide at the top, fitting tightly to the skin of the patch and the ship. He was then in no doubt that the *Glenroy* would stand up to the weather without springing the patch.

The men had a nasty job removing a lot of ruined cargo. Their work was not helped by air raids, which drove them at times to lay a smoke screen round the vessel to hide her from the raiders. All the time there was so much uncertainty as to whether Rommel would win through to Cairo that the *Glenroy* was held readiness to sink as a blockship in Alexandria Harbor. Fortunately the tide of war turned in the other direction and the *Glenroy* was spared the indignity of being sunk. She was the first ship in the annals of marine salvage to be patched with a steel patch while afloat.

Returning from the Middle East, Commander Wheeler was engaged at Cardiff one day dealing with a steamer sunk in the docks when a port official came along and was invited to lunch on the salvage ship *Forde*. Coming out of the cabin afterwards, the Commander noticed a crowd of well-dressed men gathered expectantly on the dockside.

"What's up?" asked the salvage officer.

"You're just in time to see something interesting," was the reply. "They're members of an engineering society and they've come down to see a remarkable case of a ship patched with a steel patch. She's just coming in now — the *Glenroy* — do you know anything about her?"

The salvage officer laughed. "I ought to!" he said. "I patched her."

It was a strange coincidence that he happened to be present when she came back — on one engine. Throughout the voyage her patch was so tight that she did not have to use her pumps once all the way home.

Midway through 1944 came another revolutionary development in the way of patching ships by a clever salvage officer of the Liverpool and Glasgow Salvage Association. There was nothing new in bedding down a patch on rubber, for this substance, owing to its compressibility, was particularly suitable for filling up any inequalities that existed between the ship's plates and a patch. What was new in the case of the *Frederick Bartholdi* was that rubber itself was used as a patch and not as a bed between a patch and the ship's plates.

The *Frederick Bartholdi* was a Liberty ship of 7,100 tons. She had a short life. Built at breakneck speed in 1943, she went to her death at top speed on Christmas morning of that year, stripping out her bottom on some rocks near a tiny island about five miles from Rudna Hunish, the most northerly promontory on the Isle of Skye. Her cargo alone was valued at £1,000,000, being mostly war material to be held in readiness for the invasion of France.

Among other things, she carried three sections of landing craft weighing sixty-five tons apiece which were stowed over the hatchways of three holds. Before the salvage men could get at these holds they would have to shift these sections. Had she been in dock, a hundred-ton crane would have lifted them like feathers, but how they were to be handled while she sat on the rocks was quite another matter.

There may be worse places for a ship to run aground, but not many. The natives of the Forties boast that if you want the best gales they have them. But if you wanted an unremitting dose of the worst weather that all the elements could conjure up, you need go no farther than those little islands dotted to the north of Skye and suffer what came to you.

Strong currents, high seas, and gales hit the rocks from all quarters. The Liberty ship was pinned fast under a little island that gave her no shelter. Descendants of those who have lived on Skye for untold generations admit that the weather in the Minch can be "gey bad" in winter. When those bred and born to it admit as much, it must be bad indeed.

To this inhospitable spot came that *doyen* of salvage ships, the *Ranger*, on December 27 to see what was to be done with the stranded vessel. The rocks around were a deathtrap to anything afloat. Taking careful soundings from a motor boat to locate the hidden perils and test the depth of water in the immediate vicinity, the *Ranger* made her way on top of the tide between the island and the wreck.

The immediate object of the salvage officer was to get a pump aboard the wreck to make a test. Even to experienced men pumps are not easy to handle. They are weighty and unwieldy and by the time the pump was on board the wreck the tide was ebbing fast. As the *Ranger* backed out of the danger zone, she was gripped by a rock over which she had floated safely but a short time earlier.

The cargo on the wreck was worth a million sterling. No one could say what the gear on the *Ranger* was worth. Her salvage equipment was unequaled. With it she had already saved ships and cargoes worth millions of pounds to the Allies. Now she herself was in the direst jeopardy. As the tide dropped, she listed more and more until it looked as though she would capsize. The salvage officer and crew spent anxious hours until she slowly uprighted on the rising tide and floated free without damage.

There followed a fight against weather conditions that were unrelenting. Gales boxed the compass. High seas washed over the decks of the wreck. Even when the seas moderated the after deck was still awash. For a whole month the *Ranger* stood by the wreck with a coaster, ready to take off any cargo that could be salved. Not a thing could the salvage men recover.

Many wrecks elsewhere were awaiting the attentions of the *Ranger* and her skilled crew. Leaving men to report as soon as conditions were suitable for starting work, the *Ranger* withdrew to other casualties.

To discover the full extent of the *Frederick Bartholdi's* damage took a long time. It was a question of snatching at each favorable moment to put a diver down to search and report, moving round the ship as opportunity served. So few were the opportunities that ten weeks passed before the diving survey was finished. Long before it was plain that, as a ship, the *Frederick Bartholdi* was done for. Much of her bottom plating was stripped, the shock had flung her engines out of place and broken her back, the break extending across the bottom and up each side. The bow and stern were simply held together by the deck and a few feet of plating on each side of the hull.

If ever a ship was a total loss, it was that Liberty ship. Yet owing to the importance of the war material, the salvage men received strict orders to salve the cargo. This, on the face of it, promised to be no easy job.

Weather conditions were so bad that no boat could lie alongside the wreck for six days a week. On the other hand it was essential to put men on the wreck if anything was to be saved. Their observations indicated how this difficulty might be overcome. Even when the seas were too turbulent for a boat to approach the wreck it was often possible to land men safely on the sheltered side of the island. The bow of the wreck lay about four hundred feet from the nearest point on the island, so across this gap the salvage men stretched steel ropes to form a gangway along which they could get to the ship. A further facility for getting on board was provided by hanging a steel landing net over the side up which the men could scramble when a launch could get alongside.

In normal conditions they would have loaded the cargo into coasters and left the carcase of the ship to be pounded to pieces by the seas. Another way of dealing with her would have been to sever one end from the other and refloat each part separately. But, as things were, such methods were impracticable.

After full consideration, the experts decided that the quickest way of salving the cargo was to refloat the ship as a whole and get her to a sheltered spot where the cargo could be lifted out. This entailed gaining sufficient buoyancy in the engine room and boiler rooms where the ship was broken right through the double bottom with many of the plates torn away. Then to prevent her from breaking in two while towing, they would have to adjust the weights in the bow and stern in order to close the gap in the bottom and keep the two ends pressed together.

The three sections of the landing craft were removed by raising them on jacks and launching them on launchways over the side of the ship. One section, which had to be dropped sixteen feet, made a tremendous splash as the sixty-five ton mass hit the sea, but it suffered no harm. This gave the salvors entry to three holds and allowed them to remove cargo when the weather served. They were also able to deal with some of the damage to prepare the ship for refloating.

As already mentioned, the engine room and boiler rooms were wide open to the sea through the double bottom; and the hull was split for considerable distances up each side. Pumps were therefore quite useless. The only way to refloat the wreck was to make the engine room and boiler rooms airtight down to a certain depth so that compressed air could be pumped in to force the water down through the holes in the bottom. This entailed the sealing of all top openings such as the ventilator and funnel spaces as well as the fractures down the sides of the hull.

This brought the salvors up against a difficulty which seemed to be insurmountable — how could they seal up the sides of the hull to make them airtight and at the same time allow the fractures to close up as the wreck refloated? The fracture at the bottom end was wide enough for a man to push his head through, and it narrowed as it ran up the sides of the hull until it finally joined in a plate that was buckled without being split. If an attempt were made to cover these fractures with metal, the ends of the bolts would be cut off directly the vast weights of the bow and stern moved together to close the gap, whereupon the air would escape and the wreck would sink to the bottom again.

It was this baffling puzzle which made the salvage officer hit on the idea of a rubber patch. It had never been done before, but that was no reason why it should not be tried. Rubber was flexible. It would allow the fracture to join without breaking the patch, for the rubber would simply bulge outwards and still contain the compressed air inside the ship, providing the rubber patch was properly reinforced.

While the salvage men went ahead cutting off the funnel and ventilators and sealing the apertures with steel plates to withstand the air pressure, two very long and strong rubber patches were made with the edges gripped between two metal strips. By firing bolts through these metal strips into the ship's plates the divers sealed up the fractures in the hull. They accomplished this by using a most ingenious underwater tool, the Temple-Cox submersible bolt-driving gun which fired a bolt through the metal plates and obviated the labor of drilling holes by hand.

No one, of course, could be sure how the new idea would work. All they could do was to hope for the best.

By June 19, 1944, after the *Frederick Bartholdi* had been

sitting on the rocks for six months, an attempt was made to refloat her. Running the pumps all night, the salvage team felt her floating under their feet in the morning. But a pinnacle of rock, penetrating the bottom, held her fast.

Before they could get her free, they had to lift her clear of that pinnacle. They tried forcing out the water in the ballast tanks with compressed air and found they could not get rid of the water quickly enough to empty them in one tide. Then they tried to cut holes in the tanks with underwater gas cutters to enable the water to be blown out more rapidly, but they set light to the fuel oil under the surface and had to abandon the attempt.

Still unbeaten, the divers drilled lines of holes very close together to form ten-inch squares in the tank plates, after which they blew out the squares of metal with explosives.

On the night of June 21 they boosted up the compressed air in the engine room once more to force the water out of the ballast tanks through the new vents. Two hours before high tide the ship came afloat, but the rock retained its grip on her. The post which served as a tide gauge indicated that the tide had still fifty-four inches to rise before it touched high water. The question was, Would it rise high enough to lift her over the top of that rock? The men waited with what patience they could muster, noting with satisfaction that the rubber patch was behaving exactly as the inventive salvage officer had foreseen. The tide reached its peak at nine o'clock in the morning and to their relief she floated clear and was towed to the west coast of Skye, where she was beached in a sheltered position. Here the salvors were protected from the seas while they removed her much-wanted cargo.

Although she was beyond repair, the ship was of much greater use than was obvious at first sight. She was a prefabricated ship, built up in sections. There happened at the time to be a number of Liberty ships which had come to grief in the waters of the United Kingdom. They could not be put into service again because essential parts were not available on their side of the Atlantic. Though useless as a ship, the wreck was consequently of prime importance as a store of spare parts. Accordingly, she was towed across to the Clyde where she was cannibalized and her parts used to replace the damaged parts in other Liberty ships, exactly as knocked-out British tanks were cannibalized in the western desert to keep as many in commission as possible.

The experts were not oblivious of the hazards of using a rubber patch to refloat a ship that was practically broken in half, held together by a few feet of side plating and the deck. It was a brilliant conception that demanded much faith and daring to put into practice, but it fulfilled every expectation of the salvage officer who thought of it.

The chances of using a rubber patch again seemed negligible, yet within a few months — on January 18, 1945, to be exact — a case occurred where the same ingenious idea was called upon to get another steamer over her difficulties and allow the salvage men to tow her to port. It was a foul day with winds of hurricane force. In blinding flurries of snow the hurricane caught the motor ship *Samanco* and drove her hard ashore at the entrance to Belfast Lough. The heavy seas raged about her, lifting her and ramming her on the rocks, grinding away relentlessly at her bottom, stripping heavy steel plates as though they were pages from a book.

Throughout the night the gale howled. The ship shuddered as the great waves dealt their giant blows in endless succession. Next morning the wind still blew with unabated fury as those ashore strove to establish contact with the ship by using the rocket apparatus. From the top of the cliffs the rocket sped in the heavens trailing the lifeline in its wake. The gale played uncanny tricks with rockets and lines. Drenched with spray, the little band of men on the cliff kept trying until a line caught and was held. Using that line, a stouter line was drawn across to the stranded ship to allow the breeches buoy to be rigged. In it the salvage officer from Belfast went over to the wreck about two o'clock in the afternoon of January 19 to find out what damage she had suffered.

She might have continued her voyage to India with six thousand tons of cargo in perfect safety had she been making that passage at the top of the tide. But the low tide with the gale and squalls of blinding snow brought her to her doom. The salvage officer learned that two of the forward holds were open to the sea, but the engine room had apparently escaped and a foot or two of water had penetrated the holds aft.

The real trouble was that with the forward holds flooded, the bow was pinned to the sea bed by the great weight of water, whereas the stern of the vessel remained afloat. The result was that the heavy seas began to play a devilish seesaw with the ship, each wave lifting up the stern and letting it go as it thundered against the cliffs. The bow, anchored by the weight of water, could not respond to this lifting movement. With one end immovable and the other end rising and falling with the waves, it was evident that the back of the ship would soon fracture. No ship's bottom, however strongly built, could withstand the upward strain of thousands of tons and the downward drop as the waves rolled in for hour after hour. The metal was bound to break.

It broke. There was nothing to prevent it. The danger was manifest to the salvage officer as soon as he arrived. He flooded the afterholds of the ship to keep the stern on the ground and stop the seesaw motion that was encompassing her destruction, but by then it was too late.

Badly damaged as she was, the *Samanco* presented to the salvors a simpler case than the *Frederick Bartholdi*. The two forward holds were easier to make airtight than the machinery spaces of the Liberty ship. There was no necessity to cut off funnels and ventilators and seal engine-room skylights with welded plates. It was just a case of sealing the hatches of the holds and strengthening them to withstand the air pressure that would force the water down to give the necessary buoyancy.

That was a big enough job, for each hatch had to withstand the equivalent of a load of 350 tons, which meant welding thick steel plates over the hatches and stiffening them with girders and shores so that they would not shift. But this was simpler than cutting away the top-hamper of the Liberty ship.

All they had to do to refloat the *Samanco* was to force compressed air into the damaged holds to regain buoyancy, pump out the engine room and holds aft, and seal the fractures up each side of the hull with rubber patches. It sounds so easy that the man in the street would be flabbergasted at the quantity of gear required to perform the feat. A catalogue of some of the gear was mentioned by Mr. G. R. Critchley to the Institute of Engineers and Shipbuilders in Scotland in a paper to which I am indebted for details. There were no fewer than twenty-four pumps ranging from the three-inch up to the mighty twelve-inch pump, which could swallow a child and hold a diver fast if he came close to the suction end while it was working. There were five air compressors with their air pumps, three underwater cutting sets, three portable generators, a couple of electric welding sets, submersible bolt-driving guns for bolting the rubber patches, cables of all sizes, huge balks of timber a dozen inches square and thirty or forty feet long, steel plates, steel girders, cylinders of oxygen and hydrogen, and a multiplicity of other essentials. The salvage ship was like a floating dockyard, and by the skillful use of all these salvage accessories the *Samanco* was refloated. She went ashore on January 19, 1945; by February 18 they towed her away to a nice sandy beach where she could sit without risk of further damage while her cargo was saved.

One unexpected snag appeared in the final stages of the operations. The salvors discovered that they were forcing the sea out of one hold much quicker than the other, whereas it was important to empty them at the same rate to obtain the buoyancy and balance which were necessary. Puzzled by the discrepancy, they had to unseal one of the hatchways to work down through the hold to cut a large hole low down in the hull to allow the water to be expelled from the laggard hold with greater rapidity. It occupied them for three days working for twenty-four hours on end to do this and seal the hold again.

The reason why a ship can float on compressed air with her bottom wide open to the sea may mystify many people, although the explanation is quite simple. If the upper parts and sides of the ship be made airtight and properly strengthened, the compressed air rises to the tops of the compartments where it forms a belt that increases in depth until it forces enough water out of the holes in the ship to give those compartments the buoyancy required. Instead of the sea being kept out of the ship by massive steel plates, it is kept out by this invisible belt of air. As the air is forced into the ship to increase the pressure, it expands just as it does when a boy blows up a toy balloon. Of course, the compartments of a ship cannot expand like a balloon. The steel walls and ceilings prevent the air from escaping upwards, so it expands in a downward direction and pushes the water lower. Air and water are like two giants locked together struggling for mastery. The air, held in check at the top, tries to force its way out at the bottom while the water tries to force its way in. So long as the air pressure is strong enough to neutralize the water pressure, the water can be kept out. If the air pressure is boosted too much, the excess air will escape through the holes at the bottom until the pressures of air and sea attain an equilibrium and balance each other.

Occasionally I have walked about in ordinary clothes in a sunken ship fifty or sixty feet below the surface and have picked up shingle from the sea bed and washed my hands in the sea. The ship was full of openings through which I could touch the sea; she was also full of compressed air which allowed men to work in her in absolute safety because the air pressure was high enough to withstand the sea pressure. Needless to add, if someone had opened the air-lock which gave entrance to the wreck, the sea would have expelled the air and drowned me.

Anyone wishing to understand how the salvage men work with compressed air can do so by taking a bottle, holding it vertically upside down and gently pushing the neck of the bottle into a bucket of water. The bottle may be pushed down until it is completely submerged without filling it with water. The water compresses or squeezes up the air in the bottle, but as the air cannot escape, it keeps the water out of the bottle. A diving bell works on this principle.

The astounding feature about these cases was that men could take two parts of a ship weighing thousands of tons that were literally hanging together, not by the skin of their teeth, but by the skin of a plate or two and close up the gaps to tow her away as a whole ship. Even to those who understand it most, this will always be a remarkable feat. It can be done only by a careful calculation of the weights in the various compartments of the two halves of the ship and their most delicate adjustment. If the ship has broken across the bottom, sufficient weight must be removed from the central compartments to lift them up — whether the weight be water or cargo does not matter much — while the extreme ends of bow and stern must be weighted sufficiently to sink them far enough to squeeze the two halves of the ship together and close the gap. If the ship is broken across the deck and down the sides through hogging, the weights must be adjusted to lift the extreme ends of the bow and stern slightly higher than the amidships portion of the vessel in order to press the broken parts of the deck together.

Bearing in mind that a ship may be five hundred feet or

more long, and that when she is broken across the middle the tides and seas may tend to twist each end at a different angle, some of the complications of the main problem may be realized. A slight movement at the tip of the bow, for instance, may open up a big gap in the center of the ship two or three hundred feet distant and throw the fractured plates of the bottom and double bottom out of alignment, so the salvors are compelled to balance these side movements as well as the up and down movements. To balance the two ends of a broken ship in this way demands not only the highest technical knowledge and skill, but a lifetime of experience combined with the judgment of Solomon and the patience of Job.

Never was this difficult feat more cleverly performed than by the salvors who refloated the *Frederick Bartholdi* and *Samanco*. The rubber patch devised by that fine salvage officer the late Henry Thomas for this purpose was a stroke of genius which wrought another revolution in the salvage of ships with broken backs.

In both these cases the salvage men exercised their ingenuity to prevent the ships from breaking in halves, whereas in the case of a tanker that was torpedoed off the south coast and taken into Portland the problem was to separate the two ends. The torpedo struck forward and let a flood of fuel float out to be carried away by the tide — only to be brought back again on the return tide. A survey of the damage proved to Commander Wheeler that the only way to deal with the tanker was to cut through the remaining plates that held the ends together and salve the cargo and machinery in the afterpart. The danger was that if oxyacetylene cutters were brought into play, the fuel floating on the surface would at once ignite and engulf the salvage men in a sea of flame. The salvage officer was determined to save the stern of the tanker, but he was not prepared to lose a life in doing so.

Pondering over the problem, he decided to use the forces of nature to do the job for him. Bringing an oiler alongside, he pumped out hundreds of tons of fuel from the after tanks, thus making her stern more buoyant than ever and throwing an even greater strain on the plates that were shearing through. With her stern well afloat and her bow on the bottom, he was obliged to leave the tanker for three days while he rushed off to Weymouth to attend some of the wrecks that were beached there.

During his absence another officer, looking at the tanker, decided that she could easily be cut in two by explosives. He brought along an explosives expert to consider the matter.

The expert was aghast at the suggestion. "It's impossible. If you try it you will kill half the men and there will be no end of trouble," he said bluntly.

In the face of that decision, the officer concluded that it was better to leave the tanker to be dealt with by the Chief Admiralty Salvage Officer for the Southern Area — which he did.

Up and down swung the stern, up and down under the ceaseless movement of the waves while the bow remained anchored by its weight to the bottom. For three days and nights the tough plates held out, then the metal tired and tore apart under the alternate stress and strain, exactly as Commander Wheeler anticipated.

Next day he received a telegram from the motorboat patrol officer on the spot:

REGRET TO REPORT TANKER HAS BROKEN IN TWO, THE BOW BEING SUNK AND THE STERN AFLOAT AND RIDING AT THE ANCHOR AND WIRE LAID OUT ASTERN.

Thus the salvage officer harnessed the sea to do in safety what man could accomplish only at the peril of his life. Without endangering a single man, he salved 4800 tons of oil as well as all the machinery which was duly installed in a new hull.

CHAPTER XII

Tales of Tankers

IN the far-off days of January 1941 in the distant port of Alexandria the motor vessel *Desmoulea* lay discreetly at the quayside on the eve of the most momentous voyage of her life. The *Desmoulea* was a tanker, topped with motor fuel to keep the wheels of Greece turning and the aircraft flying while the German and Bulgarian armies massed in secret for that dastardly blow which was to bring the cradle of Western Civilization under the heel of the Hun conquerors.

Without fuss the *Desmoulea* slid out of Alexandria on January 29 and headed northward for the Piraeus where her cargo was eagerly awaited. Her lookouts searched the skies and seas by day for enemy aircraft and submarines; at night she steamed without lights to avoid the attentions of any enemy lurking in the darkness. All too close to the east of her course were the Dodecanese which were ceded to Italy after the First World War and which had been turned into an ideal base for submarines and aircraft. That was the course which the *Desmoulea* had to run. The aircraft and submarines from the Dodecanese took their toll of shipping over a wide area from the north of the Aegean Sea to as far south as Suez. The tanker was right in the middle of the danger zone when a torpedo caught her in the engine room. Stopping in her tracks like a hamstrung mare, she began to heel to such an alarming degree that she threatened to founder immediately.

Giving the order to abandon ship, the captain and crew took to the boats and pulled away from the sinking tanker. As they lay off, waiting for help to reach them, they watched her keenly to see her take the last plunge. Instead, she seemed to correct the initial list and, though deep in the water, continued to remain afloat.

It had happened before, it will happen again that a ship which appeared to be in imminent danger of sinking has not gone down. So it was in this case. Despite the damage wrought by the torpedo, the tanker retained enough buoyancy to keep afloat. When the master saw this, he reboarded his ship. With some difficulty a destroyer, which had come to the rescue, took the *Desmoulea* in tow and put her ashore on a sandy bottom in Suda Bay on the northern shore of Crete.

For weeks the tides of war ebbed and flowed around her before Commander G. J. Wheeler alighted from the Sunderland flying boat on April 6, 1941, to make his desperate effort to salve the cruiser *York*. The *Desmoulea* was one of many damaged ships aground in Suda Bay, but to the salvage officer she ranked high in importance. While concentrating on the *York*, he therefore found time to devote his technical skill to *Desmoulea*, as well as many other wrecks, and gave her sufficient first aid to withstand the voyage back to Alexandria.

She was quite out of control, though it did not worry the salvage officer overmuch. Instructing two trawlers to make fast, one on each side of the ship, he used them as though they were twin screws, going ahead on one and astern on the other as required to bring her round on the right course and then, with both trawlers going ahead, steering her past the fort on Suda island and through the outer defenses of the harbor. Waiting for her outside was the patrol boat *Chekla*, which was afterwards sunk at Tobruk, ready to tow her safely back to the Suez Canal where she arrived on April 19. Thus after a lapse of three months she was brought back to her starting point.

She was laden with precious fuel for which the demand was never-ending, consequently little time was lost in coupling up and pumping out her tanks. In due course she was towed through the canal and moored in Suez Bay. Badly damaged though she was, there were still prospects of a useful life for the tanker after repairs had been made.

Her prospects were sadly diminished on August 3 when an enemy aircraft made a perfect run-in to launch a torpedo which caught the tanker just behind the bridge on the port side and exploded in two of the tanks. As if this were not bad enough, the splinters cut through the plates and flooded the next tank.

According to the law of averages this second torpedo ought to have been fatal. But it was not. Despite her terrific damage, the *Desmoulea* still stood a chance of survival. Not a great chance, perhaps, but still a chance, as her master and Commander Roberts, the naval constructor, and others agreed when the Fleet Salvage Officer arrived to diagnose the further troubles of his Suda Bay patient.

It was no good trying to get her into dry dock to tinker about with her on temporary repairs. That would have been too risky. Considering the problems of the *Desmoulea*, it seemed that her best chance, if not her sole chance, was to dock her where permanent repairs could be made and she could float away as good as new when the dock gates were opened.

Reviewing the resources on the spot, the men saw no hope of carrying out permanent repairs in Suez. They lifted their vision farther afield until they came to Bombay. Here was the nearest port where they were likely to find the facilities they wanted. Here, if anywhere, was the chance of making the *Desmoulea* whole again.

The result of their conferences was a decision to tow the *Desmoulea* to Aden, at the southern entrance of the Red Sea, and let her remain until a spell of fine weather would allow her to be towed eastwards to Bombay. Pending arrangements to tow her southwards, they decided to move her out of Suez Bay, where she was defenseless, and moor her in shallow water in the Distillery Basin at Port Tewfik.

Fifteen days later the tugs picked her up and started to tow her down the Red Sea to Aden. They crawled along in the sizzling heat for days on end. The tanker hung like a millstone on their tails, doing her best to keep them back, but they plugged steadily along to the south. It was a long tow, all of fifteen hundred miles and a bit to spare, but the tugs made it and shepherded the tanker to her moorings before steaming off on urgent business elsewhere.

The *Desmoulea* lay at Aden for week after week while the big ships dropped in from east and west for a breathing spell to allow business to be transacted and cargo and passengers embarked before they headed for Suez, the Cape, or Karachi. Twice the enemy had struck her a blow which was expected to be fatal, and twice she had escaped. Now she waited patiently to make that risky passage of another sixteen hundred and fifty miles to Bombay. Her constructors had built her with strong longitudinal bulkheads running down the length of the tanker, and on these the salvage officer largely relied to carry her safely to India in propitious weather.

Christmas came and went. On the last day of the year the tugs began to fuss around her again, the towline was adjusted, her moorings cast off and she resumed her wanderings in search of a dock that would take her in to repair the ravages of war. Hauling out of Aden, the tugs set their course due east and their unwearying screws carved a white wake in the deep blue sea as the *Desmoulea* hung sullenly behind them. Steaming steadily at five knots, they pushed on across the Indian Ocean towards Bombay. The routine was monotonous, but the tugmasters dared not let their attention wander. From time to time they conned the tanker to see that all was well with her. Averaging nearly 140 miles a day, they arrived on January 12, 1942, in Bombay where they left the *Desmoulea* and departed on further errands of mercy.

Once again the *Desmoulea* was out of luck. After being

dragged along ignominiously at the end of a line for three thousand miles, she found neither docking nor repair facilities available. She sulked at her moorings for month after month, seeing the ships coming and going, wondering how soon she would join them to feel once more the screws thrusting her prow through the seas.

At the end of April she was disturbed again by the tugs. They cast off her moorings and hauled her away to the north. Heading into the Gulf of Cambay, they skirted the coast of Kathiawar and on May 1 arrived at Bhaunagar. It was another fruitless voyage, for here again there was no dry dock available and the *Desmoulea* was left to fret at her moorings, a cripple with potentialities that could not be realized. She slumbered in the blazing heat until the tugs disturbed her once more and on November 28 towed her back to Bombay.

At last it began to look as though the fates were relenting, for after having her patience tested for a while she found herself in dry dock with men tramping about her decks and derricks swinging plates overhead and lowering them to the men on the floor of the deck. There was the clanging of metal and the babbling of tongues as the men began to heal her wounds. Her recovery was slow and when they had finished it was by no means complete, but she was patched up enough to hold 7000 tons of fuel oil.

Nearly a year passed. Then one morning the tanker beheld the tugs fussing round her again and she resumed her undignified position at the end of a towing cable instead of wandering where her master listed at the turn of her screws. She crawled behind the tugs down the Malabar coast, halted awhile at Colombo for the tugs to take breath, then followed them with what docility they could impose on her on that long leg of nearly sixteen hundred miles eastward to Singapore. Still her wanderings were not at an end, for the tugs hauled her away northward for nearly six hundred miles before they left her at

Cochin. No longer was she a proud tanker that could fetch and carry oil throughout the seven seas. She had been relegated to the status of a humble hulk for storing oil.

She served in the ranks of the fuel hulks uncomplainingly while the Japanese overran Burma and were hurled back in defeat. She served — and waited. And on January 31, 1947, after being immobilized for years, she found her days of servitude were over, for the tugs fussed around her again and started to tow her back over the old route to Singapore, to Colombo, to Bombay and Aden, then up through the furnace of the Red Sea to Suez, where she arrived on April 21, 1947.

Through the Suez Canal she was towed to Port Said, and by stages through the Mediterranean to Gibraltar, continuing her pilgrimage across the Bay of Biscay and arriving at Falmouth on July 18, 1947, still seeking a dry dock where she could rest until they turned her into a whole ship again.

Six and a half years earlier she had been beached in Suda Bay. Twice torpedoed, she had since been towed for over sixteen thousand miles to find a dry dock in which she could be permanently repaired. It was a record of tenaciousness and towing which will not easily be beaten.

There was another tanker whose name rolled round the world in paeans of praise, the *San Demetrio*. How the armed merchantman *Jervis Bay* fought the German battleship *Scheer* to save the convoy, how the *San Demetrio* with tanks full of gas was hit by shells and exploded in one devastating blast of flame as the captain and crew took to the boats, how next day the master with two or three officers and men saw the tanker afloat, how they boarded her while she was still burning fiercely and managed to subdue the fire before navigating her safely to a British port has been brilliantly told in great detail before, and will be told again so long as the traditions of the sea hold pride of place with British people. Those men who plunged into an inferno in November 1940 to write an imperishable page of salvage history were heroes all.

No minions of Hitler, but that eternal enemy of ships, a full gale, raged with such violence in January 1942 that it picked up no fewer than sixteen ocean-going merchantmen in the western approaches and tossed them on the rocky west coast of Scotland and its outlying islands as though they were cockleshells, leaving five other merchant ships with their naval escort ashore on the rocks to the north of Strangford Lough in northern Ireland. Seamen who lived through that gale will never forget it. The heavens opened, the Atlantic heaved in its wrath as the hurricane hit the ships and hurled them ashore. Among them the tanker *Laristan* under the irresistible surge of the gigantic seas was lifted over the rocks and flung hard aground on the island of Tiree, to the westward of Mull. Trapped fast with the ruthless Atlantic waves breaking about her in endless succession, her fate was apparently sealed. Yet she weathered the storm, although the risks of her breaking up were so grave that her crew had to be rescued by breeches buoy. So dangerous was her position, so difficult the approach that the wisest salvage man would have declined to hazard a guess when it would be possible to board her to learn the extent of her damage. Her chances in fact were so slender that the underwriters settled with the owners by sending them a check for a total loss — a gesture which had unexpected results, as later events proved.

As soon as was practicable, one of the salvage vessels of the Liverpool and Glasgow Salvage Association steamed to Tiree to investigate the wreck. The *Laristan* was fenced in with reefs and shoals extending for a mile and a half out to sea. It was as though Boreas had blown her on the tip of the island and dared any ship to approach her. The salvage ship, taking soundings as she went, got as close as she dared, but it was impossible to reach the wreck in the prevailing conditions. All around were hidden rocks. The breakers were so strong that the salvage ship was prudently withdrawn to a safe place to await better weather.

A wearisome week followed, with never a chance of getting

aboard. The *Laristan* was in a bad spot. Day followed day and the men were without any hope of reaching the tanker. In twenty-one days there was but one slight opportunity. The salvage officer seized it immediately. They dared not risk the salvage ship, so the salvage officer gladly risked his neck in a motorboat which put him alongside the wreck. Scrambling aboard, he made a rapid examination to glean an idea of what had happened to her, but all too soon the rising seas drove him to drop into the motorboat again. He was on board no more than two hours — two hours in twenty-one days! It emphasizes the appalling conditions in that bleak bay which was wide open to the Atlantic with nothing between its rocky fangs and the coast of Labrador.

But for the war the *Laristan* would probably have been left to be pounded to pieces by the seas. Because tankers at that time were beyond price, the officials of the Ministry of War Transport and the Admiralty, as well as representatives of the owners and underwriters, all agreed that every effort should be made to salve her. The cost was a secondary consideration compared with the ship.

The experts who studied the problem believed that she could be refloated. Her injuries were still veiled, yet they felt sure they could do the trick by pumping out the engine room and floating all the forward tanks on compressed air. They evidently expected to find the bottoms of the tanks open to the sea — a wise anticipation in view of the rocks she must have passed over to reach the gully in which she was found.

She lay with her bow about ten feet higher than her stern, and when they took soundings they found that the formation of the sea bed made it essential to maintain this trim in order to refloat her. If she were floated with her bow a foot or so higher, she would be caught on the rocks by the stern; and if she were floated with her stern a foot or so higher, the rocks would hold her by the bow. It was thus a matter of primary importance to keep her balanced at her present angle to clear the rocks and reach deep water.

All their plans, however, depended on the weather. They were slaves to the weather. In that exposed position the weather dominated everything. They could do nothing until the weather grew kinder and permitted them to work.

They looked at the wreck. She had survived a hurricane. It did not seem possible that she could suffer much more. Weighing up the difficulties with the probabilities and possibilities, the salvage experts suggested that she be left alone until finer weather came.

Meanwhile, preparations were put in hand and the experts began to puzzle out the problems. The first was to get the salvage gear on board. The wreck was not quite five hundred feet from the beach. As we know, the rocks and shoals to seaward practically barred the approach of a salvage ship, so it looked as though the gear would have to be brought overland from the island.

"That's easy!" one might think.

But it wasn't so easy after all. There would have been little trouble in landing the gear on Tiree, for the Royal Air Force had a base on the northern part of the island. Even when the gear was on the island, there remained the problem of getting it to the wreck. For one thing, the only road running in the direction of the bay where she was stranded petered out two and a half miles away. Nothing on wheels could run between the end of the road and the wreck, yet it was not feasible to carry the gear overland except on wheels. It was indeed tedious for anyone on foot to get from the road to the wreck, for it entailed scrambling over rocks and climbing up and down sand dunes. To transport the gear from the island was consequently ruled out. It could not be done.

Blocked in their approach from the land, the salvors were compelled to rely on a ship to carry their gear to the *Laristan*.

Owing to the rocks and shoals, she had of necessity to be of shallow draft, drawing no more when fully loaded than 8 feet 6 inches. It was June 10 before the seas were sufficiently calm for her to come to the wreck and allow the salvage team to lift on board the required plant, air compressors, pumps, timber, steel ropes, and the dozen and one other things which help to get a ship off the rocks.

Lacking buildings ashore in which to lodge, the men had to live in the wreck. The first thing they did was to see about making a gangway to the shore. Selecting three pinnacles of rock in a line with the wreck, they carried steel cables to these rocks and so to the shore, forming a steel suspension bridge or gangway 490 feet long. When completed it provided a means of getting ashore and conveying provisions from the island to the *Laristan*. When this link with the shore was finished, the salvage craft left them to carry on alone. Her work, for the time being, was done. Theirs was just begun. The salvors settled down to their manifold tasks with all the skill of a well-trained team. Whenever the weather served, the divers went over the side to discover her damage and help to put it right. She was cradled in a gully which made it hard to get below her bilge keels. In time they learned that her keel plate was split by a rock which had pushed up her main keel plate for a distance of about eight feet to form an arch nearly eighteen inches high.

Getting to work with explosives, the divers blasted away the rock until they could get at the damage to effect repairs. Blowing away the rock without doing further damage to the hull, they made their way under the engine room to see what had happened to the bottom. More blasting uncovered a gash in the port side about sixty-four feet long and a dozen inches wide at the widest part. Because of the way in which the plates were destroyed, they had a lot of trouble sealing it.

To deal with the damaged keel and adjacent plates, the divers were obliged to make molds which fitted perfectly over the fractures. Working to this pattern, the salvage men welded a steel patch of most unusual shape which was flat in the center and flared up on each side. Around the edges they drilled seventy-nine bolt holes. The divers manipulated the patch into place under the keel in a cradle of wire ropes, forcing it hard against the keel plates with hydraulic jacks. With the patch immovably fixed, the divers then drilled seventy-nine holes in the ship's plates to coincide with the holes in the patch and bolted the patch home. In calm water the task would not have been easy. Situated as they were, facing the open Atlantic, it was fraught with danger as well as difficulty, for there was a strong surge up the gully between the rocks and the ship's bottom which the divers found hard to cope with. It took all their physical strength as well as exceptional skill to get the patch bolted home. Another unusual patch was welded and secured in the same way.

Dirty weather played the salvage men many foul tricks. At times their crazy causeway to the shore was quite impassable: it was covered by vicious seas which marooned them on the ship. More than once their supplies ran so low that aircraft had to fly from the airfield to drop provisions on the deck to keep them going. The pilots were good shots, but sometimes a gust caught a cellophane container full of food and carried it into the sea, while the salvage men watched disgustedly. They took it all in good part; and when the divers could not work over the side they helped to fit the air connections to the flooded forward tanks in readiness to blow them out. As there were twenty-one compartments, the men had plenty to occupy their time.

Oil tankers are of course fitted with systems of pipes for various purposes. There is the pipe line through which the oil is pumped into the various tanks, with its valves for controlling each tank; there is the gas line through which air is pumped to free the tanks of deadly gas after they have been emptied; and there are pipes through which steam can be passed to clean the tanks when the oil is pumped out. Incidentally, many modern tankers are now fitted with air compressors and air lines through which compressed air can be blown into the tanks if they are holed through enemy attack or the hazards of the sea. All these pipes are fitted with valves to service the different tanks.

Naturally the salvors hoped to use one of the systems already installed in the ship for forcing compressed air into the flooded compartments and they concluded that the gas line would be most suitable for their purpose. They toiled away refitting all the valves to make sure that they were airtight; to each compartment they fitted air-pressure gauges to disclose at a glance what air pressure had been reached, for different tanks needed different pressure to vary the weight of water from one to another to attain the required trim; they fitted floats to piano wires leading through the decks to indicators which gave the depth of water in the tank — as the water was forced out, the floats sank and moved the indicators accordingly. They stopped leaks galore and performed a multiplicity of tasks to make ready for the air test.

On June 21 they coupled up their air compressors to the gas line and set them working at full speed. Their high hopes were dashed. Their faces grew grim. The work they had carried out with such zest was utterly wasted. The gas line disclosed so many unknown leaks that they could not build up the air pressure through it.

It was a bitter disappointment. Though frustrated, they were not beaten. The one certain way of insuring that their air line did not leak was to fit an entire new system of pipes, with valves to control each separate compartment. This was a big job which played havoc with their original timetable, but in due course they accomplished it. In the meantime a battery of seven pumps, ranging from three-inch electric submersible pumps to twelve-inch motor pumps, were installed in the key positions of the engine room and boiler room to pump out that part of the ship.

Gradually, as the days of July wore on, the men began to finish off their tasks, until the salvage officer was ready to make the final test. Three tugs were summoned to stand by to take the *Laristan* to the Clyde. They arrived on July 23. With the usual cussedness of nature, the weather began to play its pranks and the tugs were driven to loiter for three days before the light-draft salvage vessel could come alongside the wreck. Without the salvage ship they were helpless, for they depended on her to supply the steam through a flexible pipe to turn the tanker's winch by which they had cleverly planned to let the tanker haul herself off the rocks into the buoyed channel. It was a tortuous course, and moorings were laid so that the salvors by hauling on them could guide her in the right direction.

Early on July 27 the air compressors started to blow the water from the after tanks of the tanker while the pumps began to throw out the water from the engine room and boiler room. By 1:30 P.M., when the tide was at the ebb, all the water that could be blown or pumped out had been expelled.

It was not until four o'clock in the afternoon that the bow tanks were blown to the desired depth and the vessel regained buoyancy there. The rock, however, would not let her go. Two hours later, with the tide still rising, the stern floated off the bottom, though she was still pinned fast by that pinnacle of rock. The winch strained away at the cable to haul her off. The salvage men watched her anxiously, wondering if they were going to win or whether they would have to try again.

For another half hour the wreck kept them on tenterhooks, then the tension eased as the rising tide lifted her right off the rocky point and she floated free. There followed sixty exciting minutes during which she was manipulated into the channel and gradually worked between the reefs into deep water.

All sorts of air leakages and water leakages began to develop directly the ship was in deep water. Her trim altered. She became so unstable that she heeled right over to starboard. Then a puff of wind sent her heeling over to port. It looked as though an unexpected gust might overturn her.

As they towed her away, she began to heel more and more. Then the pumps started to choke with the debris of the ship. The prospects looked very black indeed. If they beached her, there was the possibility of disturbing those remarkable patches which had been fashioned and fastened with so much difficulty. Only in the last extremity were they prepared to do this.

In that hour of uncertainty when the tanker was heeling right over to starboard with her pumps choked, they called on the salvage ship *Ranger* to come to the rescue. The salvage crew of the *Ranger* were grappling with another wreck to the north on the adjacent island of Coll and a couple of hours after being called up the *Ranger* was on the spot. Her pumps and divers succeeded in helping the tanker over her worst trouble. She was subsequently towed halfway through the Sound of Mull where she was moored in a sheltered bay while the divers prepared her for the trip to the Clyde.

With her entry into dry dock, she gave the ship repairers many a headache. From that day all trace of the *Laristan* was expunged from the records. When the dock gates opened there came forth a fine tanker, apparently brand new, which bore on her stern the name *Empire Gulf*.

Not the least remarkable thing about this remarkable salvage case was that although the underwriters settled with the owners for a total loss, they actually made a profit of £24,000 over the wreck. At that date the Ministry of War Transport wanted tankers so badly that it bought the shattered wreck from the underwriters and had her repaired. When the balance was struck between the cost of the salvage operations and the price paid by the ministry, the underwriters found they were £24,000 to the good.

Thus the owners were satisfied, the ministry was satisfied and the underwriters were satisfied. It was a happy ending to a difficult case.

CHAPTER XIII

Trouble on Tyne

THAT troubles never come singly was fully borne out during the war when the liner *Oslofjord* hit a mine off the mouth of the Tyne. What she was worth to the Allied effort cannot be computed, but the fact that she was covered by policies of over £1,000,000 gives some indication of the value of ship and cargo to the owners.

Tynemouth harbor, so near, was too far for her to reach. The sole chance of saving ship and cargo was to run her ashore, which the captain did. The salvage men were soon busy removing cargo to lessen her draft in order to avoid fouling the channel as they took her into port. The salvage officer kept a keen eye on the Plimsoll marks as the cargo was lifted out. The ship was in an exposed position, the sea bed was soft, and he was anxious to get her to safety lest worse befell her.

Refloating her with a draft reduced to forty-two feet, he decided that the time was approaching to make the attempt to tow her into harbor. The salvors were busy on final preparations when the sound of an explosion made them look out to sea.

Another German mine had found its mark. Before their eyes a fine tanker took a list and started to sink. She was the *British Officer* and her captain made a desperate effort to bring her safely to port. Every moment she sank lower as the captain pushed her on. Just as she was being navigated between the two piers, and there seemed to be a faint prospect of getting her home, she heeled and went down.

To get her to port, the master was bound to use the fairway. As she was foundering he strove to steer her to the verge of the channel, but despite his efforts she caused some obstruction when she settled. Thus the troubles of the salvage officer who was dealing with the *Oslofjord* were multiplied by the sinking of the *British Officer*, for the clear channel that was so essential for the liner was curtailed by the wreck of the tanker. A glance at the chart told him the worst. Soundings and the port authorities confirmed that there was an insufficient depth of water in the open part of the channel to give passage to a vessel drawing forty-two feet.

With feelings that can be imagined, the salvage officer maneuvered the *Oslofjord* into a better position and put her ashore again with the intention of unloading more cargo to decrease her draft. Then the salvage men turned to the more urgent work of removing the tanker to clear the channel to port. They drove on without intermission, for to slow down the shipping on the Tyne would have had serious repercussions on the war effort.

They were beginning to make good progress with the work of refloating the tanker when a gale blew up. All that they could do was to wait for it to blow itself out. They were preparing to carry on just after the seas moderated, when another gale sprang up. The waves hurled themselves on the tanker for hour after hour, hammering away at her until they broke her back. Worse followed, for the great seas of ensuing gales finally broke the back of the liner.

All the plans of the salvage officer and the hard work of the men were brought to nought. They did their best, but the weather played with them and then the waves broke the backs of the ships. When the tale was told, all the salvage men could recover was the bow of the tanker, which they towed off to be broken up.

Day by day the masts of the *Oslofjord* sank lower in the water. The seas raged savagely about her, washing the sand in a swirl from under her keel. The massive weight of the ship had nothing solid to uphold it. She shuddered under the impact of the seas and burrowed away in the soft sand until, a twisted mass of metal, she was finally engulfed. It was a sorry end to human endeavor.

When ships behaved, the Tyne was kind to them, for she carried them to Tynemouth, North Shields, South Shields, Jarrow, and Newcastle without fuss and they could toss their hawsers over the bollards of their favorite quays and disgorge or gorge themselves with cargo until they were satiated. But if a ship got out of hand the Tyne could be very cruel and her open mouth could swallow a ship as easily as a gourmet swallows oysters. Many a fierce fight the salvage crews fought to keep the Tyne Channel clear. As thrilling as any was the struggle with the Belgian steamer *Brabo*. A ship of 3707 tons, the *Brabo* was steaming into the Tyne with a precious cargo of steel billets and scrap and wood pulp when she collided heavily with another ship and suffered such damage that she sank in the channel.

The struggle which the salvage officer and his men waged was long and unrelenting. They worked hard to salve the cargo, heaving out steel billets and sending them off to the works that were waiting to turn them into munitions. Some of the divers had eerie experiences when dealing with the paper pulp. Soaked by the sea, it naturally swelled and softened, and one day a diver, working in the hold, was completely buried in it. Fortunately those on the surface were quick to realize his predicament and another diver was sent down to help extricate him. Luckily nothing untoward happened and the trapped diver was drawn up without suffering any harm. It was not the only time that divers on the *Brabo* were trapped in this way, but after the first warning the danger was recognized, and at the first sign of the pulp caving in the divers were swiftly hauled out, none the worse for the experience.

There was one occasion when a diver owed his life to the alertness of his attendant. The latter, standing in the diving boat holding the lifeline and air pipe in his hands, thought there was something strange happening down below. He signaled to his charge and, getting no reply, promptly hauled him up. It was well that he did so, for by some extraordinary accident the intake of the air pump had slipped into the water and the pump was forcing water down into his suit instead of giving him air. The instant action of the attendant saved him, but it was a nasty experience.

Another day an attendant in the diving boat thought his charge was behaving queerly and, signaling in vain, whisked him to the surface. There was obviously something wrong with the diver, for he did not move.

Laying him on the deck, they whipped off his helmet and gave him first aid. He soon recovered in the fresh air. When they pressed him to tell them what had happened, he could give no explanation except that he had begun to feel sleepy.

Puzzling over the cause of the attack, the salvage officer happened to glance over the side and saw a motorboat under the quarter, chugging away with its exhaust puffing out fumes near the air intake of the diver. The poisonous monoxide from the exhaust of the motorboat had been sucked in by the air pump and sent down to the diver.

If ever a man had a lucky escape it was that diver, for had his attendant been a little lax he would have been lost. After that experience, the salvage officer gave orders that no motorboat was to be allowed to remain near the diving boats or salvage ship.

The *Brabo* proved to be a far bigger problem than was anticipated. In the end it was decided that the only way to deal with the sunken ship was to build a steel cofferdam round her. When this was built, she would be protected from the sea. The enclosed space in the cofferdam could then be pumped out and the men could work without interruption on repairing the damage, removing the rest of the cargo and making the necessary preparations for refloating her.

Hundreds of interlocking steel piles were brought to the scene of the wreck. A pile driver was towed down the Tyne and moored in place. The first steel pile was swung into position and set upright, not without considerable difficulty, on the exact spot where it was wanted. Then the pile driver was moved into correct alignment with the pile, the huge weight was raised and dropped down the guided ways with a crash on top of the pile until it was driven down to the required depth. With the first pile driven home, the driving of the second was not so difficult, because the edge of the first, interlocking with the edge of the second, guided it correctly into place.

It was a long job, interrupted often by bad weather. One by one the piles were driven deep into the bed and the iron fence crept slowly round the wreck. Week after week the noisy clang of the pile driver rang out from the neighborhood of the wreck as the piles were lifted into place and hammered down. Their length made them awkward to handle as they dangled from the derrick. Some slipped into place with surprising ease, others seemed to delight in refusing to connect up at the psychological moment and jigged out of place as the derrick moved slightly in the sea. Whether they ran sweetly or whether they were troublesome, they were at length coaxed into position to extend the ring of steel round the wreck.

After toiling away for six months, pushing ahead when the weather served and standing by when the gales blew up, the final pile was locked home. Gazing down on it, the operator sent the weight aloft for the last time and let it fall with a clang to give the pile a parting pat. The steel barricade against the sea was complete and the wreck lay secure in the center.

Lifting the suctions of their pumps over the cofferdam, the salvors began to reduce the depth of water over the ship. As the depth of water in the cofferdam was reduced the piles were subjected to great pressure from the sea and leaks became manifest here and there. The salvage men, watching keenly, dealt with them as they appeared. They strengthened the steel barricade with balks of timber to make it strong enough to withstand the seas.

Then they put in hand the repairs for refloating the wreck while their comrades lifted out the precious wood pulp and hauled up tons of steel scrap and steel billets to feed the furnaces along Tyneside.

At length the wreck was patched and made tight to the salvage officer's satisfaction. He looked over the *Brabo*. She was ready for refloating. The struggle and strain of these past months and the fight to build the great cofferdam in order to cheat the sea of its prey were worth while after all. The men put the finishing touches to their work. The officer checked up to assure himself that everything was ready for raising the vessel on the morrow. He was content. The difficulties had been many, but the problems were solved and tomorrow they would garner the fruits of their enterprise and hard work.

Toward evening the wind started to blow. It began to howl wickedly. The seas started to heap up at the mouth of the Tyne. All night the wind gathered force until it culminated in the worst gale on that stretch of coast for forty years.

The mighty waves, hurling themselves against the cofferdam which had seemed so strong an hour or two earlier, found the weak spots. A pile loosened and was hammered out, then another and another. The gale treated that cofferdam as though it were built of matches. When day dawned it had been wiped out, obliterated, washed away so completely that it might never have existed. Costing a fortune to build, it was destroyed in a night. With it went the last chance of salving the *Brabo*.

That is what makes marine salvage work so tricky and baffling. In peacetime a salvage concern expects and deserves a first-class award for work well done. The plans may be brilliant, the work perfectly carried out and everything that can be foreseen may be guarded against. But man must bow down to the weather. At the last moment it may snatch back a wreck for ever, and the men working on a no-result no-pay basis may lose everything when a fortune is practically within their grasp.

In wartime, of course, the nation generally pays for the work done, and the cost matters little so long as a ship can be recovered and put into service again. In these crises, ships on the sea are worth more than untold millions in the bank.

In the fullness of time when an uneasy peace descended on an exhausted and impoverished world, the salvage craft collected once more round the *Brabo* to perform their last rites. Bit by bit they cut away the top-hamper. They removed what cargo remained in the bottom of the holds. Patiently and persistently they carved out big sections of the hull to eat her away. They released the boilers and lifted them, for boilers are always useful. Very cleverly they dismantled and retrieved the engines so that they might be put to some useful purpose instead of rusting on the sea bed.

Working with explosives, they cut away all the internal girders and the outer shell of the wreck, ripping off big areas of plating for the scrap yard. All they could find of the wreck was blown away down to the sea bed. Yet that was by no means all that was left of the *Brabo*. During her long sojourn at the mouth of the Tyne she had dug deep down in the sand. Her bow had imperceptibly made its way for twenty-five feet below the level of the dredged channel. Her stern had not penetrated so deeply, though the sand had settled round it and silted up the channel to a considerable depth.

It was necessary to remove the rest of the *Brabo* to clear the channel to its original depth. This was no task for bad weather, but something to be put off until the fine weather came.

How did the salvage experts propose to go about it? Their plan was to dig the bottom of the *Brabo* out of the sea bed and carry it away in its entirety. This entailed the excavation of hundreds of tons of spoil which had consolidated around the wreck in the channel. The deposit was first broken up by the divers with powerful jets of water, after which it was removed by an airlift consisting of a big suction pipe with a valve for compressed air set inside it just above the lower end. As the compressed air gushed into the suction pipe it naturally expanded and rushed with considerable force to the surface along with a great volume of water which, as it swept strongly toward the inflow, carried with it all the silt in the immediate area. As soon as the diver had cleared one spot, he shifted the suction to clear the adjacent area.

The salvors dug away at the remains of the *Brabo* all the summer and at the onset of bad weather they left her to the mercy of the gales. With the coming of fine weather they reappeared to clear away the stuff that had washed back during the winter, and kept hard at it as long as the favorable weather lasted.

Leaving the winter gales to do their worst, they returned the following summer to round off their work. With their powerful jets the men dug a series of tunnels under the keel of the wreck. Lowering the ends of steel cables that were each capable of supporting a weight of 250 tons, they passed them through the tunnels and up to the surface on the other side of the wreck where they were secured to a lifting craft moored parallel to a similar craft so that the wreck lay between them in a cradle of slings.

Between them these lifting craft were able to raise a weight of about 2400 tons. When their tanks were flooded, they floated six feet lower in the water, so by pumping out the tanks the men were able to lift the wreck six feet off the bottom, in addition to the lift of the tide which thereabouts varied between twelve and fifteen feet, according to the season.

It is recognized salvage practice to haul the lifting wires tight at low tide and start pumping out the tanks as the tide rises, so that as soon as the wreck comes off the bottom the tugs can begin towing and take her as far as possible on one tide. If she grounds again before they can get her to dock, they repeat the process as often as necessary.

This was what the salvage men did with the bottom of the *Brabo*. Probing with their jets to insure that the keel was not held down by any consolidated material, they lifted it out of the grave it had dug for itself and towed it away to be broken up.

For the first time since the *Brabo* sank during the war, the Tyne Channel was cleared and the masters of ships could pass up and down the river in that area without fear of fouling a wreck.

CHAPTER XIV

Diving Records and Achievements

E VER since Mr. A. Catto, in a flexible suit made the world's record dive to 210 feet in 1906 during the diving experiments supervised by Professor J. S. Haldane and Dr. A. E. Boycott for the British Admiralty, the diving record has passed to and fro, but the diving specialists of the Royal Navy have seldom ceased to study the dangers and difficulties of deep diving. The result of those early experiments was a set of tables fixing the exact time which the diver could remain at certain depths and the time he must take on the way up to rid his body of the excess of nitrogen which might cause attacks of bends or diver's palsy, paralysis, and even death if the diver came up too quickly. These diving tables of the Royal Navy, the first ever formulated to make diving safe, were adopted by all the navies of the world.

Gradually our knowledge of deep diving grew and the divers were able to penetrate to greater depths in safety. But it was only by the careful application of scientific knowledge and the rigorous attention to details that divers were able to go down in flexible suits to examine the ill-fated submarine *Affray* and return to the surface without suffering any physical harm.

The Experimental Diving Unit of the Royal Navy is attached to H.M.S. *Vernon* at Portsmouth, and in seeking information about the dive in a flexible suit to 535 feet, which regained the world's record from the United States Navy in 1948, I was privileged to be conducted over the station by Commander F. C. Goodenough, then Superintendent of Diving, and his successor Commander R. F. Harland.

To expect the silent navy to make a stir about a dive to 535 feet would be to expect too much, even though it happened to be a world's record. If it became known to the British people, who still believe that Britannia rules the waves and that the British Navy is the finest in the world, the rulers of the king's navy might regard it as an indiscretion. Anyway, it was by the merest fluke that I chanced to hear about it and was given the opportunity of describing it here.

There may be well-deserved criticism about the waste of public money in many directions; but anyone familiar with the sumptuous drafting offices and experimental workshops of well-known engineering, aircraft, or motor firms would never accuse the Admiralty of wasting money on the drafting office, laboratory, and workshop of the Experimental Diving Unit. This holy of holies where the hush-hush scientific work is carried out and the prototype of any new diving gear is made for the navy was entered through the drafting office which was so compact that even the designer of a modern prefab might have learned from it how to save space. About six feet square, it served as a passage to the laboratory, workshop, and other parts of the building, and to work at his drawing board close to the doorway the draftsman was compelled to stand just inside the entrance where he was liable to be jostled by everyone passing in and out. Soon after my initial visit, however, this cramped office was transferred to the next compartment where there was ample space and fine big windows to light the work.

Two steps from the entrance was the doorway to a tiny room, perhaps eight feet by six feet, with two small flat-topped desks jammed back to back to save space, a couple of wooden chairs, a shelf for books in the right-hand corner, and a small deal table with the usual oddments. The floors were quite bare. To this little office all the intricate scientific problems of diving find their way for solution. "This is Mr. T. H. Grosvenor, our back-room boy," said Commander Goodenough.

The laboratory in the next room was a little larger — but not much. To the left, a brass-covered bench ran along one wall, at the end under the window was a lead-lined sink with running water, a deal table stood against the right-hand wall and at the end near the door was an apparatus for analyzing gases.

Scattered about the floor and bench and table were various parts of diving equipment. There was a new-type of diving helmet designed to save wear and tear on the diving suit. In a black box was a new set of shallow-water diving equipment such as the frogmen of the future may wear, and on the floor close by was a set that had been assembled for close study. A pocket on the chest of this set held two black cylinders of gas, with an emergency cylinder in a pocket immediately above them. There was the usual breathing mask through which the frogman inhaled the mixture of gases, while his exhaled breath was robbed of its poisonous carbon dioxide by passing it through a canister of soda lime carried in the center of his breathing bag on his chest. On his back were two cylinders of gas for longer dives. A clever safety device was attached to the gear on his back. It was a small leather container with four flaps, like those of an envelope, fastened by a catch at the center. This container held the leaden balls, each weighing twelve ounces, which gave him what is known as negative buoyancy to enable him to work under water and prevent him floating to the surface. To surface quickly in an emergency, the diver merely touches the lever on the front of the harness to make the four leaves of the container spring open and spill the leaden balls on the sea bed. In whatever position the diver happened to be caught, on his face, on his side, upside down or partly on his back, the four flaps of the container would fly open to release the weights and send him floating up. The one position in which the container could not work would be if he were lying directly on top of it, in which case his weight would prevent the flaps opening.

On the bench near the sink was an instrument for measuring the rate of the flow of gases under pressure. The way this difficult problem was solved was as simple as it was ingenious. To suggest that a boy blowing bubbles might help to solve an abstruse scientific problem may seem idiotic, yet it is not so silly as it sounds. Imagine a glass cylinder about two feet high and three inches in diameter with horizontal lines engraved round it at intervals of about three inches. At the bottom of the glass cylinder is a receptacle for holding liquid, and leading into it at an acute angle is a glass attachment for a gas container. When it is desired to measure the rate at which a gas flows, some of the gas is allowed to escape below the surface of the liquid. At once it does what all gases do when released under water — it rises to the surface. As it rises it expands and blows a bubble, and as this bubble of gas travels up the glass column it can be timed with a stop watch to see how long it takes to reach the various marks and touch the top.

The solution into which the gas is released is of course a soapy solution, and the gas blows a bubble to solve a scientific problem just as the boy blows a bubble to amuse himself. This brilliant idea was so simple that one wonders why it was not thought of before; but that is the way with many inventions.

In contrast to the smallness of the laboratory and original drafting office, the engineering shop was spacious and well equipped with all the machines and tools necessary to create the most intricate piece of experimental diving gear. The chief engineer, Mr. Jock Campbell, looked upon his gleaming machines with a jealous eye, and it would go hard with anyone who tried to drop a wrench in those works. Cheerful and competent, he and his assistants always managed to produce what was wanted, and if it fulfilled the tests for which it was designed no men were better pleased.

The whole science of diving is governed by pressures and gases. The deeper men dive, the greater the pressure the sea exerts on them. Unless this pressure is neutralized by the air pressure built up in their bodies and suits they would be crushed to a pulp. A diver working in perfect safety on the deck of a wreck may meet with a fatal accident by slipping to the sea bed thirty or forty feet below. Such a fall would instantly increase the pressure on his body and squeeze him to death. Many divers have been killed through such mishaps. So long as the air he breathes slightly exceeds the pressure of the sea, he is safe, but he is in grave danger if the pressure of the sea exceeds the pressure of the air reaching him.

The expression "light as air" is misleading. Air is not light. The air we breathe is very heavy. At sea level it presses on our bodies in all directions with a pressure of 14.7 pounds to the square inch. When I hold out my hand I am actually supporting about three hundredweight of air on the fingers and palm, but as the air is also supporting the back of my hand as well as pressing downward, I do not feel the weight. Our bodies are saved from being crushed by breathing air which creates an inner pressure to balance the outer pressure of the atmosphere. With the pressures balanced, we suffer no harm, and most of us from the day we are born to the day we die do not realize that air has any weight at all.

But if an inexperienced man goes into an air lock for the first time and the pressure is raised by two atmospheres, or 29.4 lbs. to the square inch, above ordinary atmospheric pressure, he will soon learn that the gentle air he breathes can exert a pressure that will kill. He will endure agonies and feel that his skull is literally being crushed in a vice. This is because the pressure outside his body increases faster than he can adjust it inside his ears. There is what the scientist terms a time lag. He suffers the worst pressure on his ear drums because they are delicate membranes which seal off the air passages in the middle ear and the strain on them makes the man feel that his head is being crushed.

This pain is so intense that I have seen the eyes of a man take on a wild glare as though he had suddenly gone mad while wondering what would happen to him next and how much more pain he could stand. Then he swallowed frantically and the mad look passed away.

In swallowing, he clicked open his two Eustachian tubes leading from the throat to the inside of each ear, and the compressed air rushed into the air spaces of the middle ear and equalized the pressure on both sides of the ear drums. With the balance restored, the pain was banished and he felt all right again.

He noticed nothing unusual in his arms and legs because they were not so sensitive to these variations in pressure, and he felt no pain in his chest because with each breath he automatically raised the pressure in the air cavities of his lungs which were well served by the large air pipes, the bronchial tubes, that passed air freely as his lungs expanded and contracted.

Men with physical defects cannot endure these increased air pressures, and I have known a man to suffer such agony in an air lock that the pressure had to be reduced to allow him to get out into the open air again. On the other hand there are men so inured to air locks and working in compressed air that they feel no symptoms at all. They have become so habituated to the changing pressures that they make the necessary adjustments instinctively. But if they missed any of the precautions which they have learned to take automatically through long usage, they would pay for their neglect.

For fifteen years, from 1915 to 1930, the United States held the deep diving record of 304 feet. Then in 1930 the Royal Navy in another series of experiments, which unfortunately cost one diver his life, carried the record to 344 feet. As a result of these experiments the extreme depth at which the crack divers of the Royal Navy could work in safety was extended to 300 feet. The diver was saved the lengthy ordeal of spending hours' on the shot rope in coming up from these great depths, and exercising for certain times at certain depths to work the excess of nitrogen out of his blood, by having a submersible decompression chamber lowered to him. Entering this through a hatch in the bottom, he was able to decompress in comfort in the company of an attendant on the way up. The submersible decompression chamber thus became an important factor in attaining these record depths.

By taking some of the nitrogen out of the air and adding extra oxygen, it was hoped to overcome the danger of bends. An excess of nitrogen may also cause the diver to suffer from another complaint known as nitrogen narcosis, which has a stupefying effect on the senses. Other experiments proved that a diver could also suffer from too much oxygen and that to send him lower than sixty feet on pure oxygen was to lay him open to the risk of oxygen poisoning, a form of intoxication. To avoid this risk and safeguard the diver on the way up, the rule was made to switch him onto breathing pure oxygen at sixty feet in order to help him expel any excess of nitrogen that had accumulated in his body during the dive.

The American deep-diving authorities sought to solve these physical problems by letting the diver breathe a mixture of oxygen and one of the lighter gases such as helium and they soon discovered that oxygen and helium gave better results than anything tried before. While there is no lack of helium in the United States, it is very scarce in England. It was therefore necessary for the Royal Navy to obtain supplies of helium from the United States before the Admiralty Experimental Diving Unit could carry out the valuable experiments in 1947–1948 during which a naval diver penetrated to the record depth of 535 feet in a flexible suit, completing his ascent in a submersible decompression chamber in accordance with modern practice.

The diving trials of 1947 were carried out in Loch Fyne at Inveraray under the direction of Captain W. O. Shelford, then Superintendent of Diving, and in a series of seventy-three dives the divers penetrated to a maximum depth of 314 feet on compressed air. One diver got his distance line entangled with the heavy weight on the shot rope and was virtually imprisoned on the bottom in such a way that he was unable to free himself. Somehow the line became twisted round the haft of his sheath knife and coiled round the bolts of the deep-diving canister of soda lime on his back. Directly he explained over the telephone that he was trapped, those on the deep-diving ship tried to lift one of the sinkers in the hope that it would release him. They could not move it. They tried to haul up the guide shot rope and that, too, was immovable, so they drew up the submersible decompression chamber to prevent the tangle from becoming worse.

Captain Shelford thereupon decided to haul up the two shot ropes with their heavy sinkers along with the entangled diver. Telling off twelve men to man the two shot ropes and the breast rope of the diver, he gave the order to heave. With a great effort they lifted the diver along with the shot ropes from the bottom at 294 feet up to 131 feet. This was a safe stop at which to give him a chance to work loose. To raise him above this depth would lift him into the danger zone and the effect upon him of the sudden decompression was problematical.

"Can you free yourself now?" he was asked over the telephone.

The diver did his best, but could not manage it.

"How are you feeling?" he was asked.

"All right," he replied.

"Stand by. We are going to haul you up farther," he was told.

They heaved on the lines again until they had lifted him to 110 feet. Then another diver went down to cut him free and the freed diver was able to do the usual diving drill until he entered the submersible decompression chamber. Thanks to the care and skill exercised by his rescuers, he escaped without ill-effects.

During these trials another diver imagined that he had carried out a dive when he was actually ten feet from the bottom. The compressed air affected him, yet he subconsciously explained all the moves of a good dive over the telephone, although those on the deep-diving ship knew that he was suspended above the bottom. He was quite all right when he was hauled up to 200 feet and had not the slightest recollection of what had happened down below. To round off the trials in 1947 seven dives were carried out on a mixture of oxygen and helium, during which a depth of 325 feet was reached.

The following year twelve new divers joined eight of the divers who had been through the trials of 1947, making a team of twenty men. They began to train for the deep-diving tests just as athletes train for any other contest, finding their undersea legs by diving in the channel on compressed air to depths of 220 feet. Then the new deep-diving ship H.M.S. *Reclaim* carried them up to Loch Fyne. Instead of penetrating to Inveraray at the head of the loch, however, they dropped anchor this time at Tarbert near the mouth of the loch. With the rains bringing down a deposit from the hills all round, the bottom of the loch was naturally muddy. Although the waters at Inveraray were very still and undisturbed, the mud was particularly sticky and the divers found the deeps so clouded with silt that nothing was visible. They were in utter darkness. Even when the submersible lamp was lowered to them they could hardly see beyond their noses, yet the light formed a friendly link with their companions on the surface and was much appreciated. Tarbert was slightly more exposed and the tidal conditions a trifle stronger, but it had the advantage that the mud on the bottom did not cling so tenaciously and the divers could see farther under the beams of the submersible lamp.

Beginning the dives on compressed air, the divers carried out 105 dives, starting at 192 feet and extending the depth until one reached 301 feet, which is regarded as the safe limit for compressed-air diving. The trials were carried through with remarkable smoothness, the only unusual incidents being that of a diver whose air pipe became twisted, another diver who was prevented from reaching the bottom by a strong tide, and a mishap which knocked away the air pipe of the submersible decompression chamber as it was being hoisted and necessitated the diver and his attendant being popped into the recompression chamber in *Reclaim*. In all cases the men suffered no harm.

As soon as the men were properly initiated into working on compressed air, the captain selected six of the finest divers to carry on trials with a mixture of oxygen and helium. They were brave men, fully aware of the risks, knowing that if the slightest slip occurred they might have to pay with their lives. They were familiar enough with diving on compressed air and knew what to expect. But helium was something new. They were not so sure of it and it is not surprising if they felt a few misgivings. Outwardly they appeared to be calm and normal, but when the medical officer came to examine them before the tests, he found that their hearts were beating a little faster. With experience, however, they discovered the advantages of the new mixture, their hearts settled down to the usual beat, and they learned to appreciate the new gas which they called "stooker juice."

Nitrogen has always been one of the diver's deadliest dangers. By using a mixture of oxygen and helium, all nitrogen was eliminated from the mixture they breathed and they were safeguarded against any illness arising from an excess of it. After the first diver had touched 240 feet, the depths were gradually increased, until on the ninth dive W. D. Barrington reached 358 feet and broke the British diving record.

In six more experiments the depths were increased until W. Bollard, who hailed from Leicester, got down to 396 feet and remained five minutes on the bottom. He told those on the surface that the dive resembled one at 120 feet on ordinary compressed air, though it was not easy to penetrate the last 100 feet.

On his next dive he got down to 455 feet without suffering any discomfort. Once again, however, he had difficulty in reaching the sea bed because he was insufficiently weighted. He reported over the telephone that he felt the same as he did when diving to 200 feet on compressed air, although he was then breathing a mixture of helium with a small percentage of oxygen that was no greater than the amount of oxygen consumed at 33 feet.

In preparing for the final dive, a little more oxygen was taken away and a little more helium added to the mixture. The diving flat of the *Reclaim* was manned. The diver was dressed in extra-warm clothing, for the divers complained of feeling the cold more when breathing helium than when breathing compressed air — in the United States divers wear electrically heated underclothing to overcome this disability.

Chief Petty Officer R. Clements who operated the diving panel throughout these trials was himself a Diver First Class, so he was very experienced and knew what to expect and what to listen for on the telephone. He held the lives of the divers in his hands, for their safety depended largely upon his skill in manipulating the panel and seeing that the pressures were properly adusted to keep them just a step in advance of the diver as he went down. The main cylinders were charged with gas at a pressure of 1800 pounds to the square inch and the pressures were varied according to the needs of the diver. An idea of the complexity of these deep-diving operations may be gained from the fact that it required a highly trained team of fifteen men to manipulate the valves and attend to the diver and the submersible decompression chamber.

After final adjustments, the diver was sent away on compressed air at 9:21 A.M., and in a minute and a half he reached the submersible decompression chamber at 165 feet, where he halted to change over from air to the oxygen and helium mixture. At 9:25 A.M. the operator on the panel heard the alteration in voice which proved that the diver had transferred to helium and the diver was sent away again. In three and a half minutes he touched the sinker on the bottom and Lieutenant H. Wardle who was in charge of the dive watched tensely as the needle of the depth gauge moved round to 535 feet, thus Bollard broke the record for a deep dive in a flexible suit and beat the American record of 440 feet by 95 feet.

Remaining on the bottom five minutes, he was hauled up to 240 feet in seven minutes. Resting there seven minutes, he was hoisted to 190 feet where he made a brief stop of a minute before being pulled a little higher to enter the submersible decompression chamber. The chamber containing the diver and his attendant was then stopped at intervals of every ten feet until it reached sixty feet. At this stage the diver was transferred from the helium mixture to pure oxygen to enable him to expel the helium from his body before starting to breathe normal air.

In seven and a half minutes this brave diver had descended deeper than any man in a flexible suit had ever been before. At this colossal depth the sea subjected him to a pressure of 260 pounds to the square inch, but as the gas being fed to him exceeded this pressure, he was protected from a danger so deadly that the slightest mishap would have killed him. While on the bottom he made no attempt to move away from the shot rope or carry out the simplest operation; but his reactions to the tests of those on the surface indicated that he remained mentally and physically efficient, which was what the group was most anxious to learn.

Whether a diver in a flexible suit will be able to perform any useful work at this great depth remains to be seen. The first American diver to penetrate over 300 feet in a flexible suit reported that his movements were much slowed down by the pressure. Nevertheless there is the possibility that as a result of these experiments the working depth of the crack British naval divers may be extended to 360 or 370 feet. I recall that once when I tried to pick up something from the sea bed during a comparatively shallow dive, I was surprised at the physical effort required to close my fingers against the pressure of the sea, as if invisible springs were holding my fingers apart. I was even more surprised by the way a gentle current turned me round in the way I did not want to go although I fought with all my strength to resist — it gave me a practical demonstration of why divers cannot work in a strong current.

In the cramped space of the submersible decompression chamber Bollard carried out the tedious stops to protect himself against bends. Then suddenly, unexpectedly, a mere thirty feet from the surface when he was breathing compressed air and they were getting him ready to enter the recompression chamber on the ship, he had an attack of bends in the elbow. They whisked the submersible decompression chamber up to the diving flat, slipped him into the recompression chamber and, boosting up the pressure to that at seventy feet, gradually lowered it to conform with the scientific tables. He was relieved at once and suffered no after effects.

As he had found it hard to get down to the bottom on his two previous dives, extra weights were added for the record dive. They made it so much easier that when he was on the bottom he reported that he felt fit enough to go down another 200 feet. The great drawback of such deep dives is the time it takes to come up again. On compressed air it is long enough, but on helium it takes even longer. It took Bollard three hours and one minute to come up from the bottom to thirty feet. Just when his ordeal seemed to be over, that attack of bends compelled him to spend another three hours and nineteen minutes in the recompression chamber.

The deep diver needs not only courage, but infinite patience.

Diving on helium brings a recognized change in the voice which must be noted by those in charge before the diver is allowed to go down. This voice change indicates that the diver has completed the transfer to helium and can safely proceed. "It was just like a breath of fresh air going through my helmet," was the way one diver described the change over to helium. At these great depths the divers cannot always think so clearly as they do on the surface, so sometimes they are given simple sums to do to enable those at the other end of the telephone to find out how they are reacting mentally. Not only physical movements, but the mind may also be slowed down in the depths, and occasionally divers have been known to carry out their diving drill automatically without remembering it.

A similar difficulty, though the cause is different, affects men at great heights. I remember one frosty night walking across Oxford Circus with the well-known British surgeon Mr. T. H. Somervell after he had attained the greatest height on Everest ever reached by man up to that time. He told me quietly how he had to breathe, or rather pant, sixteen times in making each step, and although he took a good photograph of the summit, he had not the slightest recollection of using his camera or pointing it toward the peak. As may be expected, he forgot to mention his physical sufferings and how, when practically dying on the way down, his life was saved by a fit of coughing which brought up a clot of blood that obstructed his breathing.

Despite all precautions, the diver sometimes meets with a mishap. Then anything can happen. During the search for the *Affray*, Diver Robert W. Hall was sent down at slack tide to examine a contact that had been located by the asdic at 200 feet. Slipping down the shot rope in a couple of minutes, he looked round him and saw something about ten feet away. In his efforts to identify the wreck — which was not the *Affray* — he was raised and lowered a short distance two or three times to obtain a better view. He was being pulled up three or four feet when his helmet was jolted back. As the upward pull stopped, he attempted to move and found he was caught.

"I'm fouled," he reported over the telephone, and made a partial turn to try to free himself. He was then hauled up so easily for about twenty-five feet that he thought he was free again.

Then his helmet received another jerk, his feet swung up above his head and he found himself floating upside down. Calling up for more air, he tried to get his hand behind his back to find out what was holding him. While he was striving with all his strength to get his hand to the obstruction, the extra air was blowing up his suit and making it difficult for him to move his arm at all.

There was a final jerk at his helmet and the shot rope was wrenched from his hands. He felt his suit getting bigger and harder and the dim underworld of the channel began to grow lighter while he rose rapidly feet foremost. As he moved upward he felt water running out at the back of his neck. Gathering momentum, he shot to the surface. At once eager hands whipped him on to the diving flat of *Reclaim* and thrust him into the recompression chamber under the care of the medical officer. The pressure was immediately raised to conform with the diving tables, but the diver had only the haziest notion of what occurred in the recompression chamber until the pressure was down to normal again.

The moment that he reported that he was fouled and could not free himself, six men were told off to test his lines in an effort to clear him. They gave a pull, but he remained fast. Then they tried again and pulled him up unhindered for about twenty feet. They were beginning to think they had freed him when they were halted. Shaking the lines in the hope of clearing them, they heaved together. There was a jerk as something gave.

In their efforts to free him they had pulled the telephone connection right out of his helmet and he felt the sea spurt on his neck.

Fortunately the experienced operator on the diving panel, fully alive to the danger, acted instantly to boost up the pressure of air going down to the diver. As the air pressure exceeded the pressure of the sea, it kept down the water in the diver's helmet and prevented him from being drowned. The fact that he was upside down made the compressed air inflate the legs of his diving suit before the increased pressure worked down to his helmet and expelled the water through the hole in the back of it. His suit became so stiff that he could not move a limb. That hole which nearly cost him his life was also the main factor in saving him, for it acted as a vent for the compressed air. But for that his suit would have been blown off him by the air pressure and he could not have survived.

How he was caught will never be known, but something must have slipped between his helmet and the telephone connection, and in the efforts to free him the connection was wrenched out. The obstruction was probably a rope or wire trailing from the wreck.

That experience would have put many men off diving for a long time. But not Diver Hall. Within a day or two he was diving again as though nothing had happened, and later he gazed on the *Affray* which was already covered with a greeny-brown growth of weed and small barnacles.

Lieutenant George Gosse had some blood-curdling moments in clearing the port of Bremen of mines after the war. Gosse, who belonged to the Royal Australian Volunteer Reserve, was looking for mines in the area known as the Ubersee Hafen to insure that it was safe for shipping. The mud was thick, visibility was poor, and for four days a methodical search was carried out before the first mine was found. It was a new type. The Germans alone knew how it worked. It proved to be a pressure mine, known as an "oyster," that was actuated by the extra pressure of water on a pressure bag as a ship squeezed the sea in passing.

Knowing it was essential to recover the mine intact in order to find out how it worked, Gosse went down with improvised tools to try to remove the primer and make the mine safe. He was aware that if he made the slightest slip he would be blown to pieces. Undeterred by the risk, he calmly dived, floundered about in the mud to the mine, felt about it carefully until he had located the primer and very gently withdrew it. Fixing a cable to the mine, he took the primer to the surface and gave the signal to haul away.

Just as the mine was being hauled up there came a loud crash as the detonator fired. The movement of the mine through the water probably acted on the pressure bag and fired the detonator. A second and a third time Gosse risked his life to withdraw the primer from one of these mystery mines and each time the detonator went off as the mine was being drawn up. Once, owing to the buoyancy of his suit, he had to tackle a mine when he was floating nearly upside down, yet he hung on until he had completed his task. His supreme courage won for him the George Cross.

One of his colleagues, Lieutenant P. L. F. Britnell, dived on August 5, 1945, into the Europa Hafen and found a mine buried in the mud at an angle of forty-five degrees. As the primer was underneath, and any movement of the mine would have touched it off, Britnell dug a hole in the mud until he uncovered the primer. It would not come out. He made another attempt, and another. In all he tried six times before he could get the primer out and make the mine safe. Imagine him fumbling about in the murk and mud all that time in imminent danger of the mine exploding and blotting him out of existence. Thrice he endured a similar ordeal to make three other mines safe. Today he wears the ribbon of the George Medal.

The main difficulty with which the divers had to deal in surveying the *Affray* was the strength of the tides. The divers clearing Bremen met with similar difficulties. So strong was the current at the mouth of the Weser, about four and a half knots, that the divers could not stand against it and were unable to work for more than an hour at slack water. They conducted their search between parallel lines, known as jackstays, moored to the bottom. Taking a lifeline sweep fifteen feet long, with hooks at each end, two divers snapped the hooks to the jackstays to guide them and then walked downtide until the sweep caught on something. If it proved to be a mine, they dealt with it. In this way they swept an area in and around the port of Bremen of 9,500,000 square feet and jointly covered a distance of 1500 miles, during which they were under water for 1618 hours.

Working conditions were gruesome, for the Germans had thrown into the port all the bodies of the dock workers killed during air raids. A body was found entangled in the first mine, and the divers were often driven to force their way through decaying bodies. When the mud was hard the divers were in luck, but often the slime was up to their armpits and they worked by touch in the ooze. In one case they searched an area eight times to make it safe, and concluded from the presence of a giant crater that the missing mine had been exploded by a bomb dropped by a British bomber during a raid.

These special teams of divers engaged on mine clearance were known as "P. parties." It took them six months to clear the Firth of Forth. They tackled mines from the China Sea to the Thames. They cleared the port of Amoy in China, swept up mines in Penang and Singapore and the East Indies; wherever the war impinged on the seas these gallant bands of divers swept for mines. Grappling with mines in the rivers of Burma, they wakened one morning to find that a river had changed its course and they were confronted with the task of clearing land mines from the new river bed. They risked their lives all the time to make the seas safer for ships, but their wonderful work remains virtually unknown except to those who took part in it.

The deep-diving ship H.M.S. *Reclaim* which was commissioned in June 1948 is probably the most up-to-date diving vessel in the world. Equipped with asdic and all the latest navigational and sounding apparatus, she possesses a fine sick bay, a modern laboratory with X-ray apparatus, and a galley with the newest cooking arrangements to insure that the food is well cooked and well served. Her diving flat contains a large rack holding twenty cylinders of oxygen and helium which are connected to the diving panel with its depth gauge and pressure gauges where the operator stands to control the flow of gas or compressed air to the divers, who can keep in touch with him by telephone. If one diver wishes to speak to another diver down below, the operator, by turning a switch, can link them up and check what they are saying about the work they have in hand.

A few yards from the berth of the *Reclaim* was an experimental diving tank in which selected men of the Royal Navy, after attending their lectures in the diving school, were taught to dive and carry out the drill with the shallow and ordinary diving suit before being initiated into the important work of welding metals under water.

I noticed but one difference in this tank and that in which I dived at Siebe, Gormans, under the shadow of Big Ben. The tank in which I carried out various evolutions on the instructions of the expert gazing at me through the glass windows contained clean water. The diving tank at Portsmouth was charged with muddy water to conform with the conditions the diver would have to face in the harbor.

This is as it should be.

In locating the submarine *Affray*, by the Marconi system of television from the deep-diving ship *Reclaim*, the Royal Navy performed a feat that marked a big advance in the detection of objects under water. This new development was the outcome of researches in underwater photography and cinematography carried out for three years in the Mediterranean by members of the Royal Naval Scientific Service. Much depended upon the clearness of the water and the brightness of the sun for securing the finest photographs by daylight, but in the best conditions good photographs were obtained down to depths of nearly a hundred feet at distances of up to thirty feet from the subject. Although the diver in these perfect conditions can see things between ninety and a hundred feet away, the camera will not take satisfactory photographs at more than a third of this distance, because the minute organisms suspended in the sea and the tiny bubbles of gas forever rising upward from the sea bed tend to fog the negatives.

The researches to obtain photographs at night led to the design of underwater lighting equipment in which mercury vapor lamps were found to give the best results, and these experiments in underwater photography proved to be of paramount importance when the naval scientists strove to make a television camera function at the bottom of the sea. Learning of these developments, Lieutenant Commander J. N. Bathurst, who commanded the *Reclaim*, went to see the apparatus. It seemed so promising that within a few days it was installed in his ship. After inspecting several wrecks by television over a period of three weeks, the *Reclaim* was moored over another wreck on June 14, 1951, and the television camera was prepared for lowering.

"About midday on the fourteenth of June I gave the order from my cabin to lower away," said Lieutenant Commander Bathurst in describing how he found the missing submarine. "Almost immediately I saw the rail of the conning tower hatch coming into view on the television screen. It was only necessary for us to give a few further orders for adjustment before the name on the conning tower was seen on the screen. My first reaction was to shout 'Yeoman' in order to give the yeoman of signals a message for the Commander in Chief Portsmouth that the search had eventually proved successful. There were about five people, including naval men and scientists in the cabin with me. As soon as the buzz went round the ship the whole ship's company was clambering to see for themselves the evidence of the outcome of their long and arduous efforts."

The research workers of the Royal Naval Scientific Service have thus placed in the hands of the salvage officer something new in the way of equipment that will help him to discover what he is seeking on the sea bed without endangering the life of a diver or sending down a man in an observation chamber.

CHAPTER XV

The Great Gold Hunt

For sheer drama, the adventures of the divers during the search for the gold of the Royal Mail steamer *Niagara* reached a climax that was probably not exceeded throughout the war, and the great treasure hunt carried out with such secrecy between the end of 1940 and 1941 ranks as one of the outstanding feats of marine salvage.

The *Niagara*, a steamer of 13,415 tons, had just left New Zealand on her way to Vancouver when she hit a mine about thirty miles from Whangarei Harbor in the early hours of June 19, 1940. Fortunately all the passengers and crew got away safely in the boats and counted themselves lucky to escape with their lives. But to their material losses was added a loss known only to the captain and a few high officials — the liner carried with her to the sea bed 590 ingots of gold valued at nearly £2,500,000 to pay for war material ordered in America.

Compared with the £36,000,000 more recently lost on groundnuts or the millions swallowed up by the Festival of Britain Exhibition this may seem an insignificant sum. It was about a month before the *Niagara* sank that Sir Winston Churchill became Prime Minister and none knew better than he that every ounce of gold in the British Empire was needed for our survival. A vast treasure had been engulfed by the sea and its recovery was essential — if it could be accomplished.

On this point the Bank of England was insistent, for the gold was not insured. The British Admiralty, struggling in the throes of creating a salvage organization, were unable to undertake a task which seemed to be hopeless and diplomatically declined to make the attempt. The Australian naval authorities were similarly disinclined to go treasure hunting. But within six weeks they approached Captain J. P. Williams to see whether he would tackle the task.

The difficulties were obvious. A glance at the chart told Captain Williams that the liner was down in deep water — how deep was a matter of conjecture until she was located. Certainly she was far beyond the reach of a diver in flexible suit, which meant that the only chance of recovering the gold was to adopt the methods used by the Italians to recover the gold of the *Egypt*. These methods entailed the use of a diving chamber and a special grab. The prospects of obtaining a diving chamber seemed negligible. It matched the difficulty of finding a salvage ship when every ship that could float was engaged on war work. Faced at the outset with these difficulties, and knowing full well that they were as nothing to the difficulties that would follow, Captain Williams with superb faith agreed to do his best.

To finance operations the United Salvage Syndicate was formed. At the request of the syndicate, Mr. David Isaacs of Melbourne designed a diving chamber which eventually emerged from the engineering plant as a three-ton cylinder nine feet six inches in height. Tested to withstand the pressure at a depth of a thousand feet, it had a circle of seven quartz glass windows round its mushroom top and another circle at eye level to give the diver the maximum observation above, in front, and below. Equipped with a ballast tank that could be flooded or blown out by the diver, the diving chamber had two detachable weights at its base weighing over a quarter of a ton to overcome its buoyancy and take it to the bottom. One gauge told the diver his depth, another gave the pressure of the air in the chamber which was raised slightly above ordinary pressure by releasing compressed oxygen. The diver himself wore a breathing mask connected to a canister of soda lime which absorbed the poisonous carbon dioxide from his exhaled breath and kept the air inside the chamber sweet. This diving chamber solved one of the salvage problems.

The salvage ship still had to be found. It was hopeless to look for one afloat. In the end Captain Williams came on a worn-out hulk that had been put on the mud at Auckland to finish her days. She was the old *Claymore*, a little ship of less than two hundred tons that had been stripped of her wheel and many other useful fittings. Grass sprouted from her decks, sea birds made her their home, but she was blessed with engines that would work with a little coaxing. That was enough for Captain Williams. He promptly hired the decrepit steamer, had one or two weak plates patched and went round the shipyards and docks chasing secondhand salvage gear until he found what he wanted.

By the time he had fitted out the *Claymore* and enrolled her crew, it was December, and on December 9 the steamer plodded away to the area where the *Niagara* sank. He had hand-picked his crew and had two first-class divers, Chief Diver John Johnstone and his brother Shipwright Diver William Johnstone, both of whom had been trained by the Royal Navy.

Careful calculations indicated that the wreck probably lay in the area of a square whose sides were four miles long. Marking this area of sixteen square miles with buoys, Captain Williams began the wearisome game of dragging a sweep round and round and up and down the sea bed on overlapping courses in the hope that it would catch in the wreck.

About four o'clock in the afternoon of the second day the sweep was held fast. The *Claymore* was quickly stopped to buoy the spot. But before a search could be made a gale drove the salvage ship back to Whangarei Harbor.

Christmas came and went, and it was December 29 before the chief diver settled himself in the diving chamber and was dropped to the bottom, 408 feet below, to see what the sweep had found. A short distance away he made out a dark shape resembling a rock and reported it as such.

On his way up, a wire fouled the diving chamber where no wire ought to have been, but it was cleared and the diver emerged safely on deck. A few moments afterwards a strange mass was seen within six feet of the bow. It was a weed-covered mine entangled with the cable of their anchor, not a desirable object to find so close to the ship.

With great courage, Chief Diver Johnstone donned his diving suit, had the mine lowered a few feet from the surface and struggled with a boat hook to untwist the mine from the anchor wire. A slip, a false touch, and he knew it would be the end of them all. Nevertheless he persisted until he was too worn out to continue.

They hauled him up, buoyed the anchor wire and went off to port for a mine sweeper to deal with the mine. When the *Claymore* steamed back to the spot with the sweeper, the chief diver was asked whether he would venture to make a cable from the sweeper fast to the shackle of the mine so that both ships could haul in opposite directions to snap the mooring of the mine and bring it to the surface to be blown up.

Fully aware that he was risking his life, the chief diver agreed to carry out the plan. Getting dressed, he went over the side and found the mine some feet below the bottom of the salvage ship. Grasping the wire from the sweeper in his hand, he moved up the mooring of the mine. His actions made it sway wickedly. As carefully as he could, he clutched the shackle of the mine and with an intense effort succeeded in making the cable fast.

Somehow, in some inexplicable manner, he became entangled with the horns of the mine and knew at once that he was in deadly danger. Climbing up the seaweedy surface of the mine, he came to rest on top. Time and again he collided with the plates of the ship as he strove to free himself. Ultimately he was able to clear his lines and signal for the sweeper to haul in her cable. A few moments later the mine appeared a short distance away and, after an exciting interlude, was destroyed.

If ever a man juggled with death, the diver did so then. Throughout his grim encounter the diver and all on board the salvage ship were in danger of being blasted to bits.

Early in January 1941 Captain J. W. Herd joined Captain Williams to assist the work and from then on there was the fullest co-operation between them. Their sole aim was to recover the *Niagara*'s gold and all their waking moments were concentrated to this end.

It was about ten o'clock on the morning of January 31, 1941, that the sweep of the *Claymore* caught on something big — so big that it brought the salvage ship to a halt. Both captains for the first time felt a little hopeful. The sweep was certainly round something which the *Claymore* could not shift — but that did not necessarily mean it was the lost liner.

The point was buoyed, and men were sent away in the tender to heave the lead by hand in order to sound the area. After numerous casts, during which the depths showed curious variations, the lead came up early in the afternoon with a touch of paint which provided convincing evidence that it came from the *Niagara*. On February 2 the chief diver went down in the diving chamber and confirmed it.

To locate the wreck in so short a time was a remarkable feat. It took the Italians the better part of two seasons to find the *Egypt*.

The *Niagara* lay at a depth of 438 feet, 42 feet deeper than the *Egypt*. In recovering the gold from the *Egypt* at 396 feet, the Italians had accomplished an unprecedented feat and broken all records; but from first to last it had taken them six years, clouded by the heavy loss of life when their first salvage ship *Artiglio* blew up and sank.

The salvage chiefs of the *Claymore* did not worry unduly about the extra depth. They had located the gold and were

determined to get it. The *Claymore* herself would not com-
pare with the finely fitted Italian salvage ship, but she had a
splendid crew with two crack divers who were second to
none and the latest diving chamber which the treasure hunters
felt sure would recover more than its weight in gold.

Before that stupendous task could be carried through the
salvors had to endure terrific gales, escape mines, mourn for
the men of a mine sweeper blown up nearby, and suffer all
the frustrations and disappointments which assailed them as
they grappled with the difficulties of mooring the salvage ship
exactly over the wreck and learned how to handle the diving
chamber and use their charges of gelignite to blast a way to
the gold.

On February 3, the day after the wreck was identified, the
chief diver was lowered in the diving chamber to survey the
ship, with a view to starting operations. The chamber swung
about to such an extent owing to the liveliness of the salvage
ship that the diver, to avoid the continual movement, got them
to deposit him on the deck. He was looking quietly round,
registering the parts of the ship he could see, when the diving
chamber was suddenly jerked up, slung across the wreck,
hurled over the mighty gap made by the mine and shot upside down into the mud.

The accident was caused by the salvage ship breaking a
mooring and veering in the choppy seas. Whipping up the
diving chamber as fast as they could, the others opened it to
find the diver badly cut and bruised, but thankful to escape
and quite willing to go on.

It was a terrifying experience. The fact that the diver and
diving chamber survived was a tribute to their toughness.

As soon as the strongroom of the liner was definitely
located, a cardboard model of that part of the ship was made
so that they could study how much they had to blast away
before they could get at the gold. The blasting was a laborious
and wearisome task, with the observer in the diving chamber

telephoning up to ask those on the salvage ship to swing him a yard or so to the right or left, or to raise or lower him a little. To place the charges exactly where they would cut away the wreckage required all the patience the men possessed. The man down below could only report what he saw, leaving it to those on deck to devise ways and means of surmounting the difficulties.

Gradually they blasted a hole in the ship and the voracious grab was dropped to take its big mouthful of debris and dump it out of the way. There were days when it seemed that they would never get at the gold, days when the diver could not see to work, days when gales stopped them. It appeared to be so hopeless. They wondered if the gold had been dislodged and had fallen right through the ship quite out of reach. But their spirits recovered again and they went on systematically cutting away the wreck to reach the strongroom. A gap sixty feet long was torn in the side of the ship and through two decks.

They bared the outer skin of the strongroom to find that a steel door barred their way to the gold. The ship was lying on her side. Behind the door were stacked 295 boxes of gold weighing over eight tons. There was the chance that as the ship sank and swung over, the gold had shifted, and blasting off the door might give the final touch that would hurl the treasure through the bowels of the ship to the sea bed forever.

The salvage chiefs were concerned about the size of the charge necessary to remove the door. Too powerful a charge might do grave harm when they were within reach of the treasure. They were alive to the fact that if the door fell inward on the boxes of gold it might prevent the grab from closing on them. That was a risk which they were obliged to take.

Making up a small charge, they strove for hours to drop it exactly into place. When at length they succeeded and the charge was exploded, the door vanished from the diver's ken.

That was the last week in September, and not until November 5 did the salvors observe the welcome sight of the grab emerging from the sea with the door of the strongroom literally hanging by the skin of the steel teeth. Today that steel door stands in the Melbourne office of Captain Williams as a souvenir of the treasure hunt.

Before that happy day the grab had dropped into the huge cavity with monotonous regularity, to emerge with load after load of rubbish which had gravitated from other parts of the ship into the hole. It was depressing work. Hope rose each time the grab slid under the surface and died as it spewed out its muck. October 13, 1941, may have been an unlucky day to other people, but to these men it was the luckiest day of all, for the grab brought up a box of ingots which set them cheering like mad. They had struck gold at last. The hunt was on.

The divers, peering through the windows of the diving chamber, gave their directions to the two salvage chiefs who for months sat patiently listening on the telephone and passing their orders to the crew manning the winches. With infinite care the winch men coaxed the grab into the strongroom. It was an endless game of raising and lowering the grab, swinging it this way and that until it dropped home. Sometimes it picked up a box or two of gold, but generally it vomited rubbish.

Gradually the gold began to pile up in the captain's cabin. By November 6, twenty-five days after they found the treasure, they had removed the strongroom door and had recovered gold worth over £800,000. On November 11 they were right on the mark and broke all records by salving 92 bars, worth nearly £390,000, in six hours. Eight days later, on November 19, they recovered 89 bars, and on November 20 they fished up another 48 bars. Many a young man has dreamed of streets paved with gold, but on the *Claymore* the dream was turned into reality. The gold bars were jammed so tightly on the floor of the captain's cabin that it was literally paved with gold, inches thick. It was truly an astounding sight.

Never before in salvage history had there been a treasure hunt in which the gold had been recovered so swiftly on such a scale. In thirty-seven days they lifted out of the *Niagara* gold worth over £2,000,000. It was a phenomenal feat which utterly eclipsed the record set up by the Italians when they raised the gold of the *Egypt*.

Loath to relinquish the search while any gold remained, Captain Williams and Captain Herd continued to grab for a few days, adding slowly to the spoil until the records showed that they had brought up 552 bars of gold. Somewhere down below in the strongroom or in its immediate vicinity were 38 bars of gold worth a fortune in themselves. The men got tired of lowering the grab and bringing up a load of debris. Several observers dropped right inside the cavity of the strongroom and gazed anxiously around in their efforts to locate the missing boxes of gold. The task was never easy, but in the dim light a diver thought he detected another box almost out of his range of vision. He cast an angry glance on a gleaming bar which had defied their efforts for weeks. It lay in such an awkward position that the teeth of the grab could not close on it. Dozens of times they had tried to snatch it up and dozens of times they had failed. Signaling to be hauled up, the diver made his report.

The salvage chiefs listened. They would not give up. The grab was put into operation again and under the clever direction of Diver William Johnstone it snapped up the box of gold that his brother had sensed in the distant corner.

Still they persisted. The chief diver took the place of his brother and strove valiantly to capture the bar of gold that seemed to laugh at them. Two or three times the grab came up with nothing of value. Then to the amazement of every man on board the bar of gold which had eluded them for so long dropped out of the grab to the deck.

Congratulating Chief Diver Johnstone, Captain Williams

turned to the crew and, telling them it was the end of the hunt, called for three cheers for the divers and the old ship that had served them so well.

They cheered away, but their feelings were mixed. For eleven months and three weeks they had lived together, worked together, and endured together. Underlying their quips and jests was a deep respect for each other. They had accomplished one of the greatest gold hunts in history and if their parting was tinged with regret, they had the satisfaction of knowing that they had helped to make a salvage record that will not soon be beaten.

The old *Claymore*, dragged off the mud to lift eight tons of gold from the sea bed, had had her last fling. Within a week or two of her return to port the sea crept through her worn-out plates and nearly took her to the bottom. Like her captains and crew, she had done a good job.

For nearly a year Captain Williams, Captain Herd, and the crew had risked life and limb working in a minefield while the sweepers were clearing and exploding dozens of mines. The skill and faith of the leaders and the united efforts of the crew had led to the recovery of gold valued at £2,360,000.

CHAPTER XVI

Salving a Treasure Ship

THE convoy UGS. 48 steamed out of Gibraltar Bay and headed east as the destroyers and sloops took up their positions to escort the twenty or so merchant ships safely through the Mediterranean. Montgomery had swept the enemy from North Africa, the Allied armies were clearing Italy, but the Mediterranean was not yet safe for ships to traverse unattended. Raiding aircraft were still a force to be feared. Day and night the convoy steamed until it reached the halfway house at Malta, after a quiet passage.

Gibraltar lay nearly a thousand miles behind them as they started on the run of 820 miles to Alexandria. It was a lovely summer day, bright and sunny. The air force based on Malta gave the convoy good cover to the limits of its patrol. Just as dusk was falling on Friday, August 4, 1944, and the Germans were fleeing from Florence after blowing up most of the bridges over the river Arno, a raiding force of about thirty enemy aircraft approached the ships swiftly from the north. The guns of the escorts began to blaze into the sky. The gunners on the sloop *Deptford* saw one of the enemy crumple in their barrage and plunge into the sea. The enemy pilots weaved frantically over the ships, dropping bombs and torpedoes. One pilot, making a good run in, released a torpedo that sped straight for an American Liberty ship. It struck near the stern, in No. 6 hold. There was a dull boom, and cascades of water rose on both sides of the vessel as the explosion blew an enormous hole right through her. Rarely had a ship suffered such freakish damage.

She was the *Samsylarna*, a vessel of 7100 tons. Sending out a signal to notify the naval authorities, the destroyer *Petard* drew alongside the stricken ship, while the rest of the convoy, collecting together again in due course, sped away with their escorts to the east.

The *Samsylarna* was sinking steadily by the stern. She seemed to be in so critical a state that the *Petard* took off many of the crew. All night the destroyer stood by the sinking ship. The captain and a few officers were still on board. When morning came the engine room was flooded and her stern was awash. Her plight appeared to be so hopeless that the destroyer came alongside to rescue the captain and remaining men.

The radio messages crackled out. The dire condition of the torpedoed ship was described, her exact position carefully notified. She was drifting right in the shipping lane to Alexandria, and while she remained afloat she was a source of danger to all ships using that route. It was not surprising that the question arose of whether she should be sunk by gunfire to remove the danger at the earliest moment. It seemed the most sensible thing to do. The suggestion, however, was not carried out, and the *Petard* steamed off to Alexandria with the rescued crew, leaving the wreck adrift about sixty miles north of Benghazi.

Stationed in this shattered city was the Senior Naval Officer of Cyrenaica, Commander G. C. R. Evans, R.N., who, when he took over command, found the harbor cluttered up with eighty-eight wrecks. He may have lacked technical training as a salvage officer, but he possessed in abundance all the cheerful drive that has made the Royal Navy what it is. Directing his own men, and using native labor where necessary, he raised several of the smaller craft, to clear a space in the harbor. With the most primitive gear, rigged with all the competence of a sailor, he succeeded in recovering from the bottom some sheer-legs capable of lifting seventy-five tons.

Needless to add, he found them exceedingly useful in handling heavy weights.

Bronzed and bearded, he surveyed the wrecked city. It was a desolation. Evidently he thought that things were never so bad but that they might be better. Around him was a never-ending supply of building material to be had for the taking. What was most needed in Benghazi at that moment was the magic touch of electric power so that the docks could be lighted and the wireless and radar stations wakened to life to confer their modern miracles upon the forces stationed there. These means of communication were of primary importance. If at the same time some of the living quarters could be furnished with electricity to lighten the darkness of the night, that was an amenity which would make conditions a little less onerous. Accordingly he set some of the men to work building a power station out of the debris while others attended to the necessary wiring. And when the building was finished he installed four diesel engines which, when they were started up, provided added security and comfort.

The sea drama in which the *Samsylarna* had played the leading part was revealed to Commander Evans in the wireless messages. What was not known at the moment was that she was something more than an ordinary cargo ship. She was in fact a treasure ship containing hundreds of tons of silver worth a million pounds sterling. The silver had been shipped by the Americans to the Bank of Bombay. It was a trick of Fate that she was the only ship to be hit in the whole convoy. The enemy pilot was unaware of the lucky shot he had made. The Americans were better informed, though they never knew that the luck which prevented her from foundering persisted long enough to save her from being sunk by gunfire. She was doubly lucky. Had she gone down where she was attacked, no human agency could have recovered the silver, for the sea in that area was about two hundred fathoms deep.

The wireless messages drew a quick response from the naval

authorities at Alexandria. The tug *Brigand* put to sea at once to go to the aid of the *Samsylarna* and arrived three days later at the given position. She found the torpedoed ship was still afloat. Her stern and gun platform were completely submerged, but her forward compartments held her up.

The captain of the *Brigand* circled round to study the derelict. For three days she had remained afloat. She seemed safe enough for another hour or two, with enough buoyancy forward to support her. There was, of course, always the chance that a bulkhead would collapse under the pressure and take her to the bottom with a rush. This was the risk that anyone boarding her would have to run.

The tugmaster called for volunteers to fix a tow. At once Gunner J. H. Baldwin, Leading Seaman J. C. Little, and Able Seaman C. E. Case jumped at the chance. Making everything ready, the captain brought the *Brigand* cleverly alongside the derelict and the three men leapt aboard. Their strong arms and willing hands soon hauled a towing wire over and fixed it without much difficulty.

As the tug made her bid to tow the *Samsylarna* to safety, messages began to pass between her and the naval station at Benghazi. There were no facilities in Benghazi to deal with the wreck. She was much too big to enter the harbor with its many obstructions. Commander Evans therefore expected the *Brigand* to make for Tobruk where there were better facilities for handling a ship of her size.

The captain of the *Brigand* knew quite well that if he attempted to reach Tobruk he would lose the ship before he could get home. She was too far gone to tow her a yard more than was necessary. Informing the naval officer of her condition and the depth of water she was drawing forward and aft, he asked for preparations to be made to receive her.

Commander Evans got busy. He could not take her into the harbor, so the only chance of saving her was to beach her. The point was, where could he put her? The whole coast was a mass of rocks that would have torn the bottom out of any ship coming into contact with them. He sent his men to hunt for a safe refuge. A hurried search was made along the coast in the neighborhood of Benghazi for a suitable place to beach the wreck. Eventually a small spot was located which had a sandy bottom sloping at about the same angle as the keel of the ship and there was just about enough room to take her. It was the only suitable place they could find on the coast which gave the tug enough water to allow the wreck to be towed well inshore.

The captain of the tug hoped to arrive about eight o'clock in the evening when there would have been plenty of light to put the *Samsylarna* safely ashore. The derelict, however, was so sluggish and deep in the water that he could not make more than three knots. It was obvious that he would not reach his destination until long after dark when the prospects of finding that little beach were not hopeful and the danger of wrecking the ship on the rocks loomed large.

Darkness fell, a velvety blackness that blotted out everything. Commander Evans went out to board the tug. They groped their way in the direction of that patch of sand on the sea bed. A faint light or two blinked ashore as the tug strained ahead. Then about an hour after midnight they felt the wreck take the ground. They could do no more except wait for the dawn.

When daylight came they found to their relief that they had put her ashore in the one haven on the coast where she could be beached in safety. To find that spot and place her there in the conditions that prevailed was a fine feat for Commander Evans and the captain of the *Brigand* to perform. The wreck sat there like a bird in her nest.

Commander Evans did not take long to learn that the wreck sitting on the beach was a treasure ship packed with silver. A naval guard was placed over her and Lieutenant R. B. Mc-Ausland, R.N.R., was charged with the important task of recovering the treasure. The silver was in bars that weighed about a hundredweight, and as they were brought out one by one they were stored in the old customs house.

The naval officer looked at the wreck with a critical eye. "If the tunnel doors are open we might save her," he thought. "But if they are closed, she is finished."

The commander was thinking of the propeller-tunnel running from the engine room to the stern. If the doors were open, there was nothing to prevent an inrush of water from flooding her, and by closing them it would be a simple matter to pump out the engine room and other flooded compartments.

There was but one diver available in Benghazi, and he went down to examine the tunnel doors. The *Samsylarna's* luck still held. They were open, just as Commander Evans had anticipated, and by closing them and making them watertight he knew he stood a good chance of salving the ship.

He realized full well that his whole plan depended upon pumps. That was his dilemma. All he possessed was one four-inch pump, and that was hopelessly inadequate for the task confronting him. Going over to army headquarters, he discussed his problems and met with more than sympathetic words. Such pumps as the army had were willingly placed at his disposal, while others were flown in from Tripoli and Cairo. Where the soldiers excelled themselves was in placing at his service the necessary air compressors and the invaluable portable generator which enabled Lieutenant McAusland to work the electric winches and lift out much of the cargo.

It was impossible to think about patching the immense holes that were blown right through the wreck. There were no means available in Benghazi. The most the diver could do was to cut away the loose plates and fix two or three metal patches over the smaller holes which he located, and he certainly made a good job of the work.

Pumps were not the only thing the commander needed. Many massive timbers were required to shore up the after bulkhead and the tunnel doors to insure that they did not give way under the pressure. Here again, there were no supplies in the naval stores, but there were plenty of timbers in the battered pier, so these were removed and utilized to strengthen the weak spots in the ship.

Meanwhile the recovery of the silver bars went on day and night. The stack of silver in the customs house grew so large that they had to find other places in which to store the treasure, so they dumped the bars in one or two open sheds. Men were always on guard, but nobody seemed to bother much about the silver, and the natives handled it with complete indifference.

Directly Lieutenant McAusland had recovered all the silver, an order brought along the *Lanrick* to carry it away. There were 7600 bars in the consignment, and as each was taken on board it was checked by the Americans on behalf of the consignees. The task was pushed forward with speed because everyone was anxious to get the silver safely under lock and key in Alexandria. For hour after hour the natives trotted up the gangways of the *Lanrick* and stowed the bars of silver, for hour after hour the Americans checked in the treasure bar by bar.

At length the last bar was stowed on board. The Americans checked up their lists, assured themselves that all was correct, signed a receipt and handed it over to Commander Evans. Preparations were being made for the *Lanrick* to depart when there was a warning shout and a little brown man in a white robe came out of the doorway of a tumbledown shed with another bar of silver on his shoulder, followed by another and another.

A final look round had disclosed five bars of silver lying in a dark corner where they had been overlooked. They were duly handed over to make the tally complete. Then the *Lanrick* with its cargo of silver worth a million sterling departed for Alexandria.

Toiling night and day to make her tight, the salvors managed to pump out the flooded engine room and holds of the *Samsylarna* and get her afloat by August 24. The gulf of Sirte was very treacherous, subject to the most violent storms that sprang up without warning. Having firsthand experience of the weather thereabouts, Commander Evans was anxious to get the wreck away to a safer place. Accordingly, the *Brigand* hauled her off the exposed beach and started to tow her to Alexandria, escorted by the *Kingston Cyanite*.

Within twelve hours, a terrific storm blew up which the *Samsylarna* could not have survived had she remained in her unsheltered position at Benghazi. Caught by the heavy weather as she crawled along the coast toward Tobruk, it became touch and go and it looked at times as though she would founder. The captain of the *Brigand*, however, hung on to her grimly and managed to keep her afloat until he reached Tobruk, where he was glad to take refuge, after three nerve-racking days.

Leaving the *Samsylarna* at Tobruk, the *Brigand* went off to Alexandria to collect more salvage gear, while Commander Evans sped along the coast road from Benghazi to see how the ship had weathered the storm. The gale had found one or two weak spots, and for the next week or two the work of sealing them and strengthening the vessel went forward. Eventually, in the third week of September, the *Brigand* hauled her out of Tobruk and, guarded by the escort vessel *Daybreak*, brought her to Alexandria on September 24 where she found a resting place on the beach of the old harbor. She was well out of the way and unlikely to cause further trouble to shipping.

It was here that the producer of *Antony and Cleopatra* discovered her after the war when he was seeking the correct historical setting and touches of local color for the film. To him she was more than an eyesore: she was a blot on the filmscape, obtruding into the most picturesque views where

she was not wanted. As she was as immovable as the light-
house, he was obliged to take special care to keep her off the
screen, for he knew that the most bemused filmgoers might
have considered the wreck of a Liberty ship too much of
an anachronism in Cleopatra's day.

CHAPTER XVII

Clearing Cape Cod Canal

I F Great Britain was fortunate in possessing the Liverpool
and Glasgow Salvage Association with its plant and trained
personnel on which to build her naval salvage organization
at the outbreak of war, the United States were no less fortunate in possessing the Merritt-Chapman and Scott Corporation with its salvage ships equipped and manned ready to be
taken over under contract when the Japanese struck their
blow at Pearl Harbor. The biggest marine salvage concern
in the world, the corporation handled practically all the marine
salvage jobs in the United States. It operated from five salvage
stations along the Eastern seaboard with five salvage ships
whose trained crews and salvage masters were as competent
as their British counterparts.

Unhappily, when the tides of war lapped the American
shore, the United States Navy was no more fitted to deal with
the merchant ships slaughtered by the German submarines
than the British Admiralty had been. Two years earlier, within a week or two of that sunny Sunday of September 3, 1939,
when Hitler unleashed the war in Europe, high-ranking American naval officers had the wisdom to recognize their un-
preparedness. The result was that in the following month of
October Commander W. A. Sullivan of the United States
Navy was sent over to England to learn how the British
Admiralty were facing their grave difficulties. Needless to
add, Commander Sullivan was warmly welcomed. Nothing
concerning marine salvage was hidden from him. He went
over existing salvage ships and noted how few they were.

He discussed technicalities with the most brilliant British salvage officers and realized that they possessed the experience and knowledge to tackle any salvage problem that came their way. He chatted with them about their equipment and learned what they preferred and why; and as he went around seeing things for himself he found no lack of salvage knowledge, but a lack of everything else — pumps, salvage ships, lifting craft, balks of timber, all the essentials without which the trained salvage men would remain helpless beside a stricken ship that could easily be patched and taken into dock if they were properly equipped.

He went into financial questions with the Admiralty and learned what arrangements the Salvage Department had made with the commercial salvage concerns upon whom the nation depended; he discovered how they were tackling the major task of training men and refitting old ships that would have to serve until new ones could be built. Everything concerning marine salvage was studied by him with a keen mind. Having completed his mission, he returned to the United States and reported faithfully on all he had seen and done. In due course Commander Sullivan, whose skillful supervision of marine salvage later led to his promotion to commodore, joined the Bureau of Ships in the Navy Department as Supervisor of Salvage.

His report set in train inquiries to find out what facilities existed in the United States to deal with any marine salvage problems that would arise in the event of war. The results were disquieting. The United States Navy was in the same position as the Royal Navy. Apart from the naval specialists and craft for dealing with sunken submarines, it had neither trained crews nor salvage ships to cope with the certain war losses of merchant shipping.

In a *Short History of the Naval Salvage Service*, the Bureau of Ships of the United States Navy Department gives a summary of Commander Sullivan's mission to England:

His report indicated that the chief difficulties encountered by the British had been the shortage of trained men, salvage ships, and salvage gear, rather than technical problems. These difficulties had been augmented by the general ignorance of salvage problems exhibited by various shipowners, masters, naval officers, and some government officials. Ordinarily, the British Navy does not participate in salvage. When naval ships require it, the work is done by salvage organizations, but in time of war the Navy takes over the control of these commercial organizations and co-ordinates and directs their efforts.

Here is official confirmation from an independent source of Great Britain's hazardous position when the conflict began. After mentioning how Commodore Sullivan joined the Bureau of Ships, the history continues:

On June 9, 1941, the Bureau reported to the Secretary of the Navy that a detailed survey of the existing salvage facilities in the United States disclosed them to be wholly inadequate to most war-time requirements. It pointed out that only one commercial salvage company then operating in the United States, Merritt-Chapman and Scott Corporation of New York, was equipped to do coastwise or offshore salvage work on vessels of any size. This company operated five salvage vessels, all of which were stationed along the east coast.

The United States Navy followed the example of the British Admiralty and took over on terms that yielded rich financial rewards to the American people the whole of this fine salvage organization that had been built up and sustained by private enterprise. The corporation's directors and salvage masters who had been grappling with salvage problems all their lives thereupon brought all their experience and energies to bear on the gigantic task of salving the ships that came to grief in American waters as well as farther afield. More salvage ships were built and men were trained for the Navy Salvage Service, and they had their work cut out when the German submarines attacked the defenseless merchant ships along the east coast of the United States. The salvage ships themselves were unarmed, but several put up a bluff by painting some of the spars used for lifting purposes to represent guns, and more than one submarine, surfacing close by, did a crash dive at sight of the dummy guns.

Nevertheless the enemy wrought terrible havoc all along the eastern seaboard and gave the Navy Salvage Service more than enough to do. Their achievements were impressive, for during the war they salved 498 ships and cargoes worth 675,640,967 dollars, and gave effective help to over two hundred more ships. The terms on which the salvage service worked specified that all salvage awards should be paid into the United States Treasury, which had received three and a half million dollars from this source by 1947. At that time claims worth two million dollars were still unsettled, but these have since been dealt with. The most astounding fact that pays the highest tribute to the efficiency and patriotism of the Merritt-Chapman and Scott Corporation as well as to the United States Navy is that during the six years from 1942 to 1947 when the Navy Salvage Service was engaged on this arduous task the total operating costs were no more than 19,450,745 dollars.

The first impact of war revealed to the United States Navy the necessity of protecting the coastal shipping. All the merchant ships trading in the Caribbean Sea and along the Atlantic seaboard were subject to attack. Notwithstanding that Commander Sullivan had made a full disclosure of the unprepared state of Great Britain in 1939 to cope with the marine salvage problem and had emphasized the inability of the United States to deal with a similar problem, little was done to remedy the deficiencies before the blow fell. At that hour the fifty old American destroyers and ten other craft so generously loaned to Great Britain for convoy work would have been a godsend.

The United States was hard pressed. Her people were restive under the penalties exacted by the German submarines. Her naval escorts were too few to guard all the ships moving round her coasts. In that dire emergency Great Britain promptly came to her aid by the loan of thirty-six antisubmarine vessels, with their trained crews, to help to stem the attack.

As quickly as possible the United States built up a system of convoys for its coastal traffic, extending the range as the escort vessels became available. The merchant ships steaming from the South to ports in the North were collected at certain places and escorted to their destinations, altering course as required to avoid any submarines that were known to be operating in the vicinity. Similarly, the ships moving from North to South were gathered together at points named by the authorities and were then convoyed down the coast through the danger zones.

About sixty miles southeast of Boston was the southern shore of Cape Cod Bay with a narrow neck of land terminating in Cape Cod forming a great arc swinging back nearly thirty miles to the north in the direction of Boston. Within these waters the merchant ships were fairly safe; but if they ventured outside into the open Atlantic to the east of Cape Cod on their journey to the South they were compelled to run the risk of attack by German submarines. To shorten the journey South and save time and money, a canal known as the Cape Cod Canal was driven long ago through the southern end of that narrow neck of land and it now assumed an overriding importance. It became a savior of ships, and all those ships which were not too big to pass through it were sent that way.

The morning of June 28, 1942, was very foggy; it was the sort of day that all shipmasters hate. The captain of the steamship *Stephen R. Jones* did not like it. She was a vessel of 4387 tons, with a length of 354 feet, a beam of 49 feet, and a depth of 27 feet 4 inches. The master's instructions were to go through the Cape Cod Canal, which in normal circumstances would have been an easy thing to do. But in that fog which blanketed everything it was not so easy. As the captain felt his way cautiously along the canal with a cargo of coal, the ship gave a sudden jar and scraped horribly along the bank.

The bank was riprap, composed of rough stones that tore at the ship's plates and caused a rush of water into the forward hold that took her down by the head. The crew toiled like demons under the master's orders to secure the stern to the bank so that the passage of the canal would not be imperiled. They could not control her. Despite their efforts the stern swung away from the bank. The changing tide exerted its full force against the ship's hull and pushed her broadside across the canal, snapping her moorings as though they were cotton threads, and in a little while she capsized and sank.

It was a disaster which drove ships of any size to make the dangerous voyage to the east of Cape Cod and brave the worst that the German submarines could do. The canal hereabouts was 500 feet wide at the bottom, so a narrow passage still remained unobstructed. But the wreck acted like a dam in the canal and the swift current, heaping up, flooded the roads on both sides.

The United States Army Engineers were quickly on the scene. The difficulties of clearing the wreck out of the way were obvious at a glance. Losing no time, they got in touch with the Navy Salvage Service. With equal promptitude the Supervisor of Salvage, Commodore W. A. Sullivan, and Captain W. N. Davis, one of the salvage officers of the Merritt-Chapman and Scott Corporation, took their seats in an airplane and were flown north to the canal.

They surveyed the wreck. The water was racing by so swiftly that no diver could work in it. Had any diver been sent down he would have been swept away at once. The only chance that a diver would have to work at all was at the ebb of the tide when he might expect to toil for fifteen minutes, or with luck for half an hour, before the tide began to flow. Normally the salvors would have cut up the wreck with their underwater cutters and carried the bits away. Under existing conditions it would have taken them eight months to do this. The normal method was unthinkable. It was essential to clear the canal with the least possible delay. Not a day, not an hour could be lost. While the canal was closed to the bigger ships, the German submarines might reap a rich harvest.

The salvage experts examined the passage between the wreck and the bank. That was something to the good. A few small ships might still creep past if they exercised caution. As for the wreck, they decided in the end to blow her to pieces with charges of explosives right down to the bed of the canal. The only snag to this plan was that a short distance away the Bourne Bridge was carried across the canal on its piers and they were afraid that the detonation of the charges would set up an underwater shock that might damage the piers and even lead to the collapse of the bridge. This was a risk they were driven to accept. There was no other way out for them.

Collecting the essential equipment and other necessary material, the salvors rushed it to the canal. Some crack divers along with experts who had specialized in cutting up wrecks by explosives were flown to the spot. They celebrated Independence Day on July 4 by placing a charge of 350 pounds of blasting gelatine and setting it off in the early morning, while keeping a watch to see what effect it had on the bridge. As no ill-effects were visible, they increased the size of the next charge, and on the following day they decided to use a charge of 1450 pounds, or well over half a ton. It was the biggest charge used on the job and the piers of the bridge suffered no harm.

Every day at slack water the divers went down to place a charge, and every day the wreck was gradually cut down. The size of the charges varied according to the work they had to do, the smallest charge used being 170 pounds. On July

11, a bare week after starting the job, the wreck was blasted away sufficiently to give 28 feet of water over the stern jutting across the canal. This was deep enough to give passage to the small ships which took the fullest advantage of it. Pushing on with all their energy, the experts cut down the wreck another four feet for a distance of 150 feet along the hull in the next four days, to give a depth of 32 feet over this portion of the wreck. It gave larger vessels a chance of making the passage. This was remarkable progress.

There was still much to do and the American experts did it. By July 31 they had shattered the wreck to such an extent that at low tide there was more than 32 feet of water over any fragments that remained.

All the time the canal authorities were grappling with the difficulties of working ships past the obstruction. They handled the vessels with such skill that about thirty a day were successfully passed through and during the month they managed 722. It was an astonishing feat that reveals more than anything else the vital importance of the canal at that time.

The War Department engineer in charge of the Cape Cod Canal wrote to Merritt-Chapman & Scott on August 8, 1942: "Lend-lease cargoes are now going through our Canal in body and the shipping people are again happy."

CHAPTER XVIII

The Mysterious Phoenix

M ORE fabulous than the phoenix of ancient days was the
Phoenix of the war years, and the mystery of the old
was as nothing compared with the mystery surrounding the
new.

When Winston Churchill suggested that a harbor should be
built out of blockships to assist in the invasion of Gallipoli in
the First World War, he anticipated by a generation his instructions to set in train the plans for building a harbor for
the invasion of France in the Second World War. Without a
harbor, the invasion of the Continent was impossible. All the
Continental ports were so strongly fortified by the enemy as
to render their capture doubtful. Even if captured, the destruction of the port installations was likely to be so complete
as to make the port unusable for those first critical days when
it would have been fatal to impede the free flow of troops and
munitions.

In the circumstances the only alternative was for the in-
vading armies to take a ready-made port with them and plant
it in their own time in their own place. It had to be a harbor
built up of units that would float and could be towed to the
coast of France and dropped into place like the pieces of a
jigsaw puzzle, a port as big as Dover, capable of landing about
10,000 tons of supplies and munitions a day. That was what
the invasion of France demanded and what the engineering
genius of the Allies produced. It was the Mulberry Harbor,
a greater wonder of the world than the Great Pyramids or the
Hanging Gardens of Babylon.

The conception and building of this vast project would provide the subject for several books. I can only touch on aspects of the general problem that are of exceptional interest and reveal how at the climax the whole project was placed in jeopardy and saved by one of the war's luckiest accidents.

The Germans were not the only enemy to be taken into account in the invasion of France: wind and wave were enemies no less powerful, all the more to be feared because their reactions could never definitely be forecast. So far as the wind was concerned, the most the experts could do was to study the conditions over a long period and select the month and the days which human experience had proved to be most relatively calm; so far as waves were concerned, the scientist could at least do something positive and carry out a series of experiments to try to discover the best means of breaking them up and mitigating their worst effects upon any breakwater that might be installed.

Accordingly, Dr. F. H. Todd, who was Principal Scientific Officer of the Ship Division, was asked in September 1943 to carry out a series of experiments with Mr. J. L. Kent in the tanks at the National Physical Laboratory at Teddington to find the best form of structure for breaking up waves and reducing their force. Many models were made, some with latticework faces, some with upright bars, some presenting a perpendicular wall to the waves, others presenting an angle; some had holes in them in the form of slots, others in the form of squares; some were filled with brushwood to absorb the force of the waves — all that science could suggest and ingenuity devise was subjected to a most exhaustive series of tests by Dr. Todd and his colleagues at Teddington. By October 9, 1943, Dr. Todd had committed his initial findings to paper and placed them before the War Office, where Brigadier Sir Bruce G. White was in charge of this great undertaking. By the end of November the experiments were finished and the results were under official consideration.

Fast as Dr. Todd was compelled to work to obtain his results, the men who built the units were expected to work faster. They were asked to build all the units for two prefabricated harbors in six months and have everything completed by May 1944. On the face of it, this was a physical impossibility. A harbor normally takes years to build, yet the British and United States Governments were demanding that two modern harbors with all their working facilities be provided within six months, one for British and the other for American use. Anyone who said it could not be done might claim to have reason on his side.

The plan for each harbor embodied two floating breakwaters known as Bombardons, with a big fixed outer breakwater to form a harbor in which Liberty and other ships could shelter and unload. Before the invasion of France could be undertaken it was necessary to build six miles of units to form the fixed breakwaters. These units were aptly named Phoenix units by someone with a taste for the classics, for he sensed that out of their sinking and ultimate destruction a new France would arise, as well as a new Norway, Belgium, Netherlands, and Denmark.

Such a prodigious task in so short a time had never before been considered by man. Colossal was an apt description. It was quite new, fraught with immense difficulties that called for the collection of mountains of sand and cement and steel rods before it could be carried through. Brigadier Bruce White, as he was in those exciting days before he was knighted, had the good sense to realize that to tie up the project in red tape and attempt to push it through the slow official channels of peacetime would be to court disaster. He had six months to produce six miles of breakwater that would float over to France. It had to be done, and the only way to do it was, as Kipling remarked, to fill each unforgiving minute with work well done.

There were certain main factors which these experts had

to bear in mind. The breakwater would have to be built of concrete units, or caissons, which would float, strong enough to stand up to seas of a certain height and capable of being towed by tugs at four and a half knots, with a deck and shelter for a crew. Above all, these units had to be simple to make, so that they could be constructed rapidly with the available labor.

That it was a super-top-secret goes without saying, and the town clerk of an area where land was requisitioned confessed to me that he had not the slightest idea of the underlying purposes which suddenly brought into the district an army of two thousand men and gave the local authorities trouble galore in finding accommodation for them. We have heard a lot about the best-kept secrets of the war; but there can be no doubt that the Mulberry Harbor was one. The thousands of men engaged in making and pouring concrete all over the country knew that they were building something, but what it was they did not know, so they could not tell. The men who knew were discretion itself.

The result of the deliberations of all the civil engineers and scientists and designers was a mighty concrete box 204 feet long by 56 feet wide and 60 feet high. This big box had a central wall running down its whole length, with other walls running from side to side to divide it into twenty-two compartments. Holes were left at the bases of alternate cross walls so that water could flow from one compartment to the other and each of these twin compartments was fitted with a five-inch valve with its outlet on the outer face of the caisson near the floor and a twelve-inch valve about twelve feet up the wall. The whole structure had to be sunk quickly directly it was in place, for the men engaged on the operation would probably be under attack and a Phoenix towering say forty feet out of the water presented a vast target compared with one that was showing no more than six feet above the surface when it was submerged at high tide. These valves were therefore necessary to fill the box rapidly with sea water and alternatively to pump out the compartments if necessary.

The top part of the unit was set back to allow a six-foot gangway all round, bollards were placed at each end to take towing wires, and as the units had to be towed considerable distances the ends were swim-shaped or boat-shaped to ease the strain on the unit. "They looked like gigantic Noah's Arks," was how an engineer engaged on the job described them to me.

To allow for the variations of the depths of water at Arromanches with the sea shallowing at each end of the breakwater, the units varied in height from forty to sixty feet, the bottoms and outer walls of the former being twelve inches thick and the latter fifteen inches thick.

While the engineers were working out strains and stresses and the thickness of outer and interior walls, as well as a multitude of other things, the scientists were carrying out experiments in the tanks at Teddington to fix many points of the design. Brigadier White gave the experts their heads and they excelled themselves. By an incredible feat, the team of experts working under the direction of the War Office calculated the stability of the units, thickness of walls, strength of reinforcement, and the whole weight of the structure in two days. These calculations embraced all the six types of unit that were planned. The drawing staff at the War Office, spurred by this record, put up another by completing all the detailed drawings in two weeks. These were astonishing performances.

The Ministry of Supply was saddled with the problem of finding 20,000 men to carry out the work, arranging for the sand and grit and cement to make half a million tons of concrete and with squeezing out of the overworked steel works 50,000 tons of steel rods, all cut to the required lengths, which in the aggregate would extend for hundreds of miles.

While various aspects of this great undertaking were still being worked out, twenty-four of our best-known contractors were instructed in December to begin the job. There was not a day to spare if the Phoenix units were to be constructed in time. To them fell the multitudinous problems of finding the skilled men to supervise the work, of preparing and organizing the sites, scouring their workshops for the most suitable tackle, arranging for the feeding of the men in canteens and seeing that they were properly billeted.

At first it was thought that all the Phoenix units could be made in the various docks around the country. This idea proved to be illusory. There were not enough docks available.

Taking the disappointment in their stride, the contractors set their excavators to work scooping out great basins along the banks of the Thames, moving mountains of soil, laying acres of concrete floors with their supporting walls of brick or concrete to enable them to work on forty units at the same time. When the units were built to a certain height, they let the Thames flow into their basins so that the structures could be floated out and completed according to plan.

In one case, owing to the flooded condition of the land, deep drainage pits had to be dug from which the water could be pumped to dry out the site and enable the concrete floor to be laid over the firm bed of gravel beneath. The first Phoenix unit was thereupon built to the requisite height, the water was let in and the unit gently floated out.

The site was then pumped dry again and another unit was built. The water was let in as before, but instead of floating, the unit stood there as immovable as though it had been cast in the solid earth. The water lapped round its walls, but the structure sat tight.

Imagine the surprise of the builders! It ought to have floated exactly like the first unit. They wondered what had gone wrong. For a while they eyed it anxiously as they puzzled over the problem. Then they began to smile. "It will float in about two hours," they said.

They were right. In about two hours it became buoyant and was floated away.

The reason why it refused to float was quite simple. The bed of gravel beneath the site had been robbed of all its water by pumping, and not until the water had percolated through the gravel and flooded the space between the lower water level and the floor of the basin could the unit become buoyant.

The contractors launched their first Phoenix unit on March 28, 1944, and by April 27 they had launched seven. In all, twenty-three units were successfully launched.

It was planned to moor all these Phoenix units in safe places until they were wanted on D-Day. As the work progressed, however, it was discovered that there were not enough moorings in the country to allow this to be done. To counter this setback it was decided to sink the units in parking places and raise them as they were wanted. This meant a considerable increase in the work, but it was the only way to overcome the lack of moorings.

The utmost care was of course necessary in selecting the parking places. It was first of all important to insure that the units would be safe from enemy air attacks. Then it was essential to see that the area selected was flat and free from rocks, for if a unit settled down on a rock it might break its back. And there was the question of mud. A slight deposit was not very objectionable, but if the units sank too deeply into mud there might be considerable difficulty in raising them at the very moment when everything had to work smoothly to insure the success of the invasion. As the units were completed they were towed to these parking places and sunk by crews of Royal Engineers who had been specially trained for this operation on models in the tanks at the National Physical Laboratory at Teddington.

The sinking of a Phoenix unit was by no means simple. The flooding of the various compartments had to be carefully controlled to make sure that the unit sank on an even keel. If it developed a list in sinking, the men were shown by the experiments with the models at Teddington how to correct it by letting more water into other compartments. The original plan visualized that the only chance the men would get of sinking Phoenix units was when they were taken over to the French coast after D-Day, so the construction of models for the training of the men was important.

By parking the units on the sea bed near Selsey and Littlestone, the men were able to see how the actual units behaved when they were being sunk. The parking therefore served as a dress rehearsal for the great day. But the parking added one complication to the general problem. It meant that all the units had to be pumped out and raised before they could be towed to the French coast. And this in turn meant that pumps must be provided for as big a pumping effort as was ever undertaken. To cope with this prodigious task, the necessary pumps on floats were duly ordered to be made ready for the day. The proposal was to moor on each side of a Phoenix unit a pumping float mounted either with a nine-inch pump or two four-inch pumps.

The Admiralty had suggested sinking a line of fifteen blockships to form the backbone of the fixed breakwater. The naval authorities stressed the advantage of the ships that could cross the channel under their own steam and be sunk with a minimum of effort to create an initial shelter for the landing piers and invasion craft. The navy was accordingly charged with the task of preparing and sinking the blockships and getting the floating breakwaters, or Bombardons, into place.

The War Office was responsible for raising the Phoenix units for Admiralty tugs to tow across to the other side where the units were to be handed over to other tugs with crews specially trained to maneuver them into place, after which specially trained crews of Royal Engineers and naval men were to take charge and sink them. The plans were brilliantly made. Everything that could possibly be foreseen was provided for. The men were properly trained to conjure up a harbor in a few days where previously there was but a bleak seashore.

The Admiralty Salvage Department was also preparing for D-Day in its own way. The salvage officers knew quite well that the invasion could not take place without shipping casualties, and very quietly they gathered together within easy reach of the other side all the salvage ships and gear they could lay their hands on. Tucked away unobtrusively on the south coast were four lifting craft capable of giving a thousand tons of buoyancy to a ship in need; the salvage ships made a sizeable fleet of eighteen; the salvage men collected twenty pontoons which lame ducks might need to keep them afloat; steel plates for patches were loaded onto supply ships, special quick-setting cement by the ton, steel girders, long balks of massive timber, underwater cutters, diving suits, air compressors, portable generators, all the paraphernalia that would enable the salvage men to save a ship and bring her safely home, not forgetting pumps of all sizes, with great coils of lifting and towing wires from four inches to eight inches in diameter, the latter capable of supporting a weight of 150 tons without breaking.

Apart from the vast amount of work entailed in mobilizing this fleet of salvage ships and auxiliary craft with all the gear for the coming invasion, the salvage men had their hands full in other directions, for ships did not cease to get into trouble because the invasion was in the offing. The normal calls for help were met with the usual promptitude, and towards the end of May an urgent demand reached the salvage department to refloat a craft that was aground in the neighborhood of Littlehampton.

Straightaway a salvage ship was dispatched to the scene.

The eyes of the crew nearly popped out of their heads in amazement. This was the most peculiar craft they had ever been called upon to succor. It was, of course, a Phoenix unit. In the course of being towed to the parking ground at Selsey it had snapped its towing wires and broken away from the tugs. Resembling an enormous block of flats without windows, this gray mass of concrete drifted along while the seas lapped its sides and the men on the tugs struggled to get it under control again. The wind blowing on that vast area of concrete made matters worse. The crews of the tugs did their best to stop the drift shorewards, but the unit was out of hand and eventually it grounded and sank inshore, a disaster which led to the call for help.

Until it happened, the salvage section had no knowledge whatsoever of these enormous concrete boxes or the part they were designed to play in the invasion. A few miles along the coast was the parking ground at Selsey where eighty of the units were sunk to await the day when they would be refloated and towed over to build up the harbor at Arromanches, the British harbor known as Mulberry B to distinguish it from the American harbor at St. Laurent known as Mulberry A, which came to grief in the great storm that raged a fortnight after D-Day.

Everything was poised in readiness. The invasion was about to be launched. It merely needed the word of General Eisenhower to set all the forces in motion. An army of men, toiling night and day to build the Phoenix units, had completed their spectacular task in 150 days. The crews of the tugs were trained to handle them; the units were waiting to be refloated. But the floating pumps on which the whole operation depended were not ready. These pumps were a vital link in the invasion plan. They were the missing link. The nightmare rush to produce this modern miracle of a floating harbor had made it impossible to complete the pumping floats in time. It was a desperate situation. Unless the Phoenix units were raised and towed to France to form that breakwater, no one could foretell the consequences. At the worst there was the awful danger that the entire invasion plan might go awry. As soon as the Admiralty Salvage Section discovered the facts, they stepped into the breach. The realization of all that was at stake was overwhelming. Without hesitation the salvage men undertook the biggest pumping operation their department had ever faced. It was something for which they were quite unprepared, something they had not anticipated.

Somehow, somewhere, they had to collect salvage officers and ships and pumps with all the other auxiliary craft to pick these giant concrete boxes off the sea bed and send them floating away across the channel. Telephones buzzed, messages went out, dispatch riders in their crash helmets purred along the roads. And from various harbors salvage ships began to converge on Selsey where the sea swirled about the sunken units. One by one they arrived, interspersed with a coaster or two. A motor launch turned up, then came one or two tugs towing lighters, and so it went on until a fleet of eight salvage ships was assembled with all the other odd craft without which the work could not be done.

When Eisenhower gave his signal on D-Day, Tuesday, June 6, 1944, the salvage officers jumped to their jobs and set the pumps going for all they were worth. None but those on the spot can know with what relief they felt the first gigantic structure move in its bed and gradually rise higher and higher until it dwarfed the tugs which eventually towed it away beyond the horizon. Phoenix units were queer things to handle, but the refloating of the first one taught them a trick or two about handling the second, which was refloated in due course and towed away. It is a matter of interest to know that only four blockships had been put down in their places at Arromanches when the first two Phoenix units arrived and were successfully sunk in position.

Night and day the pumping went on. A mighty unit stirred

in its bed of shingle, gradually came up, was connected with the tugs and towed away. Some of the smaller units constructed on the foreshores weighed 3000 tons, the larger weighed 6000 tons, but small and large came alike to the salvage men who toiled without rest to back up the troops fighting for a foothold in France.

Lifting their portable pumps up to the gangways of the units, the salvors dropped the suctions down into the compartments and sent the water gushing back into the sea. Ten, twenty, thirty, forty units were raised. Nothing could stop the devoted salvage men — except the weather. When it came on to blow, they fumed at their impotence. But a gale slamming against the side of such an enormous structure would have rendered it unmanageable, so they were forced to exercise patience until the wind subsided and the seas abated.

They found that one mighty unit had been launched and parked in such haste that the interior still contained some of the scaffolding used in the building. It made them rather anxious about the safety of their precious pumps. When they managed to get another afloat, they saw that all their labor was wasted, for there was no possibility of towing it to Arromanches, so they had to let it sink. Such disappointments, however, were few and far between. Of the eighty Phoenix units parked at Selsey, no more than three displayed faults which compelled the salvors to sink them again.

By June 19 the salvage crews near Selsey had raised no fewer than sixty-five Phoenix units. It was a magnificent effort, all the more so when it is borne in mind that there were three days when the weather was so bad that pumping operations had to be stopped. At that time twenty-five Phoenix units had been sunk to build up the outer breakwater at Arromanches while twenty-eight units had been sunk in position at St. Laurent.

Then ominous skies with a fall in the barometer heralded an unexpected gale which broke with a fury that was seldom experienced at that time of year on the French coast. It raged from June 19 to June 22. The worst gale for forty years, with waves running twelve and fifteen feet high, it overturned the blockships at St. Laurent and utterly destroyed twenty-five out of the twenty-eight Phoenix units, thus forcing the construction of a harbor at St. Laurent to be abandoned.

The Calvados shoal gave some protection to the harbor at Arromanches which lost only five Phoenix units in the heavy seas. As soon as the gale died down, the movement of these huge concrete boxes across the channel was resumed until the entire breakwater with its protective arm at each end was completed a month after the first assault craft poured their troops on the French beaches to start the invasion. At one time in the early days the situation of the troops ashore became so critical that only someone with second sight could have forecast the outcome had it not been possible to land eight hundred tons of ammunition — just in time.

That is why the grounding of the Phoenix unit at Little-hampton which seemed at the time something of a catastrophe turned out to be one of the luckiest accidents of the war.